A Pembrokeshire Childhood
in the 1950s

Phil Carradice

AMBERLEY

About the Author

Phil Carradice is one of Wales' best-known writers. He is a novelist, poet and historian and has written over forty books. For Amberley he recently wrote *First World War in the Air* and *The Great War*, while his latest novel is *The Black Chair*. He broadcasts regularly on BBC radio and television and presents the BBC Radio Wales history programme *The Past Master*. He also writes a regular weekly blog for the BBC Wales website.

Acknowledgements

Most of the photographs in this book come from the author's personal collection – most but not all. Thanks have to be given to the following for the loan of several images:

Anne Hughes
Judith Scourfield
Roger McCallum
John Evans
Trudy Carradice

First published 2012

Amberley Publishing
The Hill, Stroud
Gloucestershire, GL5 4EP

www.amberley-books.com

British Library Cataloguing in Publication Data.
A catalogue record for this book is available from the British Library.

ISBN 978 1 4456 1311 6 (print)
978 1 4456 1320 8 (e-book)

Typeset in 10pt on 12pt Sabon.
Typesetting and Origination by Amberley Publishing.
Printed in the UK.

Contents

Part One

Chapter One
Early Years

As Dylan Thomas once said, the memories of childhood have no order. Or maybe it wasn't Dylan Thomas at all; maybe it was Wynford Vaughan Thomas in his one-man show where he played the part of the infamous Welsh bard. Either way, it's a true enough statement.

When you try to get some sort of order to your memories, all those evocations of past events, they come rolling off the page like tumbleweed. In case you don't know what tumbleweed is, it's the bushes of dead scrub that come blowing down the streets of western towns in those interminable John Wayne or Randolph Scott films that we always seemed to be watching during my childhood days.

Characters, major and minor, stride on and off the stage but not necessarily in the right place or at the right moment in time. I suppose that mixing up of people and places is what makes the attempt to describe your childhood so fascinating.

It's only with hindsight that you even begin to see that what you lived through was history in the making, as surely and as certainly as if you found yourself in the middle of an earthquake or the Great Plague.

The post-war period, the 1940s, '50s and '60s, was a time of great social, political and economic change, arguably a period that was more revolutionary than any other in our history. It was an amazing time in which to grow up.

Living as we did in the west Wales town of Pembroke Dock, I was always aware of being on the edge of the country and almost on the fringes of society. We were, quite simply, a long way from the centre of things, a little community that, before the days of easy transport and immediate communication, seemed remote and almost forgotten by virtually everyone – apart from those who lived there.

I don't think I was particularly conscious of my 'Welshness', certainly not in those early days. I suppose it was only when I was nine or ten and my class at school was taught the National Anthem – in both Welsh and English – that I became aware a place called Wales even existed; or that there was a thing called 'Welshness'.

If anything, it was Scotland that, to begin with, was my guiding star. My father was a Scot who had come to Pembroke Dock during the war and his tales of high mountain passes, deep glens and salmon rivers where you could catch one of those giant fish with your bare hands – as long as you were still and patient enough – were what intrigued me.

I wanted to be Davie Balfour fleeing from the Redcoats or Richard Hannay, hunted through the heather by the watchers of the Black Stone. I'd never heard of Owain Glyndwr or Llewellyn the Last, never knew that the King Arthur I read about so avidly in the big leather copy of *Tales of the Round Table* I kept on my bedroom bookshelf actually had a Welsh origin and background.

All of my childhood and adolescence, Dimond Street, the main shopping street of Pembroke Dock, was a busy and populous place. In this view from the 1950s, the shops on the north side of the street are well protected from the sun by large canvas awnings – even Woolworth's.

We were never taught about such people at school. When I did, finally, become aware of my birthright, it wasn't Wales so much as Pembrokeshire that first impressed on my consciousness.

I guess that awareness was helped by a short film made, incongruously enough, by one of the oil companies that were, even then, beginning to move in and despoil Milford Haven. *Pembrokeshire, My County* gave me not just pleasure in the place where I lived, but absolute and all-consuming pride. Very quickly, it became Pembrokeshire first, Wales second.

I suppose that stance is now tied up with a degree of defensiveness. I must have heard it a hundred times, the comment, 'Oh, Pembrokeshire. That's not really Wales, is it? It's all English down there.' And nothing has really changed, no matter how fervent I have become in my Welshness. It's still Pembrokeshire first.

Good stories should always have what novelists call 'The three Ps' – place, people and problems. People and problems are variables; different people have different takes or interpretations on everything, but place remains constant.

Growing up in Pembroke Dock – as Dylan once said about Swansea 'an ugly, lovely town' if ever there was one – was an experience I would never want to change or lose. It's a cliché but, like all clichés, a truism and I know that the place made me what I am.

A strange mixture of rural and urban environments, it was the ideal location for a young boy to take those first, tentative steps towards adolescence and adulthood. In the '40s, '50s and '60s, those amazing days of change and liberation, there was no better place to be.

We never used the word 'suburb' about any part of Pembroke Dock but that's what Pennar, where I lived, really was. Like Bufferland, Llanreath and Llanion, it was a small community on the edge of the town. Green countryside was never more than a few hundred yards away while over the top of Tregenna's Hill waited the town and all its wonderland of shops and stores.

Pembroke Dock stood, and still stands, on a low shelf of land on the southern shore of Milford Haven, about 6 or 7 miles from the mouth of the estuary. Backed by a steep ridge, it is bounded by water; Milford Haven and the Cleddau River to the north, Pembroke River to the south.

It was the water and the sheltered open land that brought the Admiralty to this region at the beginning of the nineteenth century. In 1814 they created a dockyard here – the only Royal Naval dockyard in Wales. It was an establishment that existed for over a hundred years and produced some of the greatest warships in Queen Victoria's navy.

The town that grew up in the shadow of the dockyard was a vibrant and exciting one, a place that quickly acquired a sense of importance way beyond the practicalities of the situation. Wide streets and tall, elegant buildings were the mark of the town, the only truly industrial community in the whole of Pembrokeshire – an industrial community set within the heart of green countryside.

The old medieval town and borough of Pembroke lay just 2 miles to the south-east. With its huge and imposing castle – originally a motte-and-bailey structure built by Arnulph de Montgomery in 1093 – it was the area's first nod to military history. Henry Tudor had been born there and the town and castle were once besieged by no less a person than Oliver Cromwell himself.

Milford Haven was supposedly called the finest natural harbour in the world – by no less a figure than Admiral Horatio Nelson. This view shows one of the oil refineries that, from the 1960s onwards, littered the estuary sides.

This aerial view of Pembroke Dock gives a good indication of the size of the town and its location on the Milford Haven estuary. Hobbs Point, complete with sheer legs, lies on the left of the picture while the open land at the bottom right is part of the Barrack Hill.

Pennar, a small community to the south of Pembroke Dock, was a quiet, self-contained suburb. This postcard view shows the single-storey cottages in Owen Street, originally built for dockyard workers. Military Road and most of the streets in Lower Pennar were lined with similar dwellings.

We enjoyed the fame and the reputation of the castle but, as we grew older, it was the municipal and sporting rivalries between Pembroke and Pembroke Dock that most exercised our imaginations and, inevitably, our muscles.

Pembroke Dock might have been the young pretender as far as military might was concerned but its position and significance were always suspect. Our wonderful dockyard was, to put it simply, in the wrong place at the wrong time. Isolated at the far end of west Wales, without viable technology and the communications network to sustain it, as the twentieth century unfolded it quickly became clear that the yards could not hope to survive for long.

The dockyard was ideal when France was Britain's traditional enemy and the place was building wooden warships. The thirteen covered building slips to cater for these enormous vessels made our dockyard the largest in the country, but the yards could never hope to compete once iron and steel became the main building materials for warships and the threat of Bismarck's Germany became a reality.

The dockyard closed in 1926, the Royal Fleet Auxilliary oil tanker *Oleander* being the last vessel built in the yards. Battleships and royal yachts had been created there but the last vessel to be built was a humble oil tanker; a ship that was later sunk during the Norway Campaign of 1940.

By the time I came into the world the dockyard had, for many years, been reduced to what was called a care and maintenance standard – apart from a brief resurgence during the war – and the town was left without purpose or design. Nevertheless, the old slipways and buildings remained a constant reminder of the glory that had once been Pembroke Dock.

For many years after the war the Admiralty maintained a small presence in the western part of the dockyard, establishing and running a mooring and marine salvage depot there. If it employed a couple of dozen men it was lucky and, in reality, that depot was only ever a tiny reflection of what had once been.

Private building or repair yards were also established along the waterfront in the post-war days, RS *Hayes* in the old dockyard itself, Hancocks Shipbuilding Company in Front Street. My uncle Jim worked for Hayes for a while, cycling down Tregenna's Hill each day and then making his way back up the steep slope each evening.

Both companies repaired and even built a few ships, Hancocks producing the *Cleddau King* and *Cleddau Queen* ferry boats for Pembrokeshire County Council. In 1955 Dick Hayes and his firm converted a German cargo vessel into a cable layer, re-named *Ocean Layer*, and went on to build several trawlers for the Milford Haven fishing fleet.

It was a last desperate attempt to keep shipbuilding alive in Pembroke Dock, but by the early 1970s the industry was dead. Pembroke Dock – my town, my home – had been created to build ships. Now its reason for existence had been taken away.

I was born on a Sunday in October 1947 at No. 41 Military Road in Pennar. It was a home birth, as most were in those days, a bed for my mother having been moved into what was always called the back, as opposed to the front, room. They were the best, the 'poshest' rooms in the house, reserved for Christmas, Easter and for events like funerals – and my imminent arrival.

The Royal Fleet Auxilliary tanker *Oleander*, the last ship to be built in Pembroke Dockyard. She was sunk in the Norway Campaign of 1940 during the Second World War.

A group of workmen on their tea break at the private shipbuilding firm of R. S. Hayes, established in the old dockyard after the closure of the Royal Naval yards in 1926. My uncle Jim is the young man seated second from the left.

My mother was attended or helped by her mother and a few aunts who were experienced in things like giving birth. My father's role in the affair was to sit biting his nails in the kitchen and then bury the afterbirth in the garden.

The house was a large, rambling old building, built in the 1860s, standing on a wide road that led to open fields and, at the far end, overlooking the Haven, a collection of buildings which were originally an underwater mining depot for the army. By the time I arrived the place had already been converted into a barracks for the Royal Engineers.

When No. 41 was first built, it was detached and standing in its own solitary splendour but, over the years, a long line of single-storey cottages – of a style found in most other dockyard towns across Britain – had been built along the road and one of these soon found itself attached to the western flank of our house.

Grandfather and his family were farmers and hauliers, many of whom had gradually moved into other trades over the years, trades that were considerably more profitable than tilling the land and involved a lot less work. The family still farmed, in an off-hand sort of way, but it was more a hobby than a lifestyle. Indeed, the old farmyard – largely disused by the early war years – was still owned by the family and located just twenty yards down the road from No. 41.

Jack Carradice, my father, had been born in Elgin in the far north-east of Scotland and came to Pembroke Dock after the Dunkirk evacuation. Forget Winston Churchill and his 'fight them on the beaches' nonsense, Dad said, the discontent and anger among the defeated soldiers after the debacle of Dunkirk was endemic.

Dad was always fond of prophesying that if those in charge had been unwise enough to send the soldiers home on leave, most of them would never have come back! And so they despatched Dad and his unit as far away from their native land as it was possible to get – Pembrokeshire in the far west of Wales.

Encamped at West Pennar in the bitterly cold winter of 1940–41, Dad's friend Jonty Linney told him that he had distant relatives in nearby Pembroke Dock. It was a long

The *Ocean Layer*, converted from a German cargo vessel into a cable layer by the firm of R. S. Hayes, is shown here, just off Carr Jetty in the old dockyard. A tug pulls her free of the jetty before the new vessel can begin her sea trials.

The Motor Vessel *Kirtondike*, again built by the firm of R. S. Hayes in the old dockyard, slides into the water on the day of her launch. Private yards like those of Dick Hayes provided the last vestiges of shipbuilding in the town.

Staff Sergeant Jack Carradice, seated left in the front row, just before his discharge from the army.

Above left: My mother – and me – in the back yard of No. 41 Military Road. The photograph shows more of Uncle Freddie's house next door than it does of No. 41 but it gives a good indication of the size and height of the buildings.

Above right: Mum, on leave from the WAAF, in the back garden of No. 41. The identity of the dog remains unknown!

walk, never easy at the best of times, damned difficult with snow on the ground, but the welcome, he said, would surely be worth it.

They made the journey, only to be greeted on the doorstep of 41 Military Road by my future grandfather – who had never heard a guttural Scottish accent before.

'Spies!' he shouted as he grabbed a pitchfork from the lobby. 'Dirty German spies!' He chased the two soldiers down the road for almost half a mile before his wife caught up with him and told him she was expecting visitors.

'Just you go and get them back,' she said.

Of course, every time Grandfather got within 50 yards of Britain's finest they took to their heels and ran again. It was at least an hour before he managed to persuade them he meant no harm and when they did finally make it back to No. 41 Dad immediately fell in love with Mary, the daughter of the house. The rest, as they say, is history.

It was a long and somewhat distant courtship. In due course, Dad went off to India and Burma – to defeat the Japanese, single-handed, he said – but wrote regularly and kept in touch with his beloved Mary.

After the war he returned to Pembroke Dock, married her and underwent emergency training as a teacher at the Heath Training College in Cardiff. He spent the rest of his working life, first, as an art teacher, then deputy and then, for a brief period, head teacher of the Coronation Secondary Modern School in the town. Over the years Jack, as he was invariably known by everyone, became a famous figure in Pembroke Dock.

The war had a profound effect on Pembroke Dock. It was, perhaps, something of a mixed blessing as between 1939 and 1945 the place was once again a dockyard town, the old yards having been reopened as a repair base for the duration of the war. RAF Coastal Command also operated out of part of the old dockyard, sending huge Sunderland and Catalina flying boats on long range missions out over the Atlantic. Large numbers of soldiers were quartered in and around the town at one of three large and echoing sets of barracks.

What all that meant, of course, was that the town was a prime target for German aerial attacks. Pembroke Dock was bombed many times between 1940 and 1943, over 200 residents being killed, hundreds more seriously injured. The damage to the streets and houses was immense. The dockyard and flying boat base were, in contrast, quite untouched.

Some of my earliest memories are of bombed-out houses, deep pockets of destruction and desolation that survived several years after the war ended, stretching back from the roadways. Whenever we walked into town we would pass these strangely evocative open wounds, jagged gaps like missing teeth in streets that were otherwise full, regular and pristine.

Always there were children playing in the rubble or, often, just standing there, staring and watching us pass by. Cats and something more sinister – mice and rats, perhaps – scuttled away at our approach, but the children remained, staring and challenging.

As I grew the town slowly began to put itself back together after the torment of the war years. It was, I suppose, like most other British towns in the '40s and '50s as, slowly, a rebuilding programme began to fill in those gaps in the terraces.

For the full length of my childhood, it seemed, there were piles of builders' sand and chippings lying outside so many of the houses. We played for hours in that sand, whoever it belonged to, fashioning roadways for our Dinky cars or building forts for our lead soldiers.

With so many houses damaged and demolished, the Town Council – like many other councils across Britain – was forced to build estates of prefabs. The most notable one in Pembroke Dock was the Britannia Estate at Bufferland.

These prefabricated little houses were compact and totally self-contained, offering a degree of comfort that was unheard of in the pre-war days. They were warm and fitted with things like oil cloth, foldable tables and built-in cupboards. Originally intended to last just ten years, the Bufferland prefabs were still there – and still occupied – in the early 1970s. People loved them.

Relatives abounded in Military Road. My mother's family, the Phillips clan, was large and had once been quite wealthy. That wealth had long gone by the '40s and '50s, God only knows where, but for most of my childhood there were still houses full of Phillips family members stationed along the full length of Military Road. Aunty Della, Aunty Lizzie, Uncle Jim, Aunty Ave, Aunty Jean and so many others – they were an integral and essential part of growing up.

I never regarded this proliferation of relatives as anything other than normal. It was before the days of geographical mobility, a time when people tended to be born in, live in and then die in the same town, maybe even the same house. At the time it was

Pembroke Dock became the largest flying boat base in the world, known throughout the Air Force as PD. Many aircraft were based there but the most famous – and the one that will be forever associated with the town – was the giant Sunderland.

Above left: Workmen repairing bomb damage to a house in Commercial Row in the years immediately after the war.

Above right: Pembroke Dock suffered terribly at the hands of the German Air Force, hundreds of houses being damaged or destroyed. This view shows one blitzed house at the corner of Gwyther Street and Apley Terrace, severely damaged in a raid on the night of 11/12 May 1941. Pembroke Dock station can be seen in the background.

One of many prefabs built by the government in the immediate post-war years. They were intended to last no more than ten years but many were still inhabited in the 1970s.

A worn image of the Phillips clan, out in force, at a family wedding. From left to right: Mum, Aunty Jean and Aunty Della.

expected and accepted, the way things were. Only with hindsight can I appreciate the warmth and security such close family contact offered.

Next door to us sat Uncle Freddie and his family, his wife Eva and four children, all older than my sisters and I. Freddie was a Town and County Councillor who was famous – perhaps infamous might be a better description – in Pembroke Dock and the county of Pembrokeshire.

Once, having learned that bodies had been moved in the town cemetery – in order to allow some Town Councillor to be buried overlooking the river – he called a public meeting to expose the scandal. Favours were called in and Freddie's motion of censure was defeated. Finger pointing towards the Heavens, Freddie stormed off the podium at the end of the meeting. 'This weekend,' he thundered, 'some of you will be laying flowers on the graves of your loved ones. My advice to you is don't.' He paused and gazed at the stunned spectators. 'Don't,' he continued. 'Because you don't know which rotten bugger you'll be laying them on!'

Perhaps more interesting to me, however, was the fact that Uncle Freddie had gone down in history as the town's first civilian casualty of the war.

At the top of Military Road, just before the mining depot and Royal Engineers Barracks, stood eighteen large oil tanks. In 1940 they held vital fuel oil for the Royal Navy escort vessels. Freddie and my grandfather farmed the land around those oil tanks, little thinking that they might spell disaster for them and the town.

On 19 August 1940, as Freddie and Ronnie, my grandfather, were threshing corn in the field opposite the tanks, three German Dornier bombers swept in over the coast and deposited a stick of bombs onto their target. Only one hit the mark but it was enough. The tank exploded in a mass of flames.

The blast picked up Freddie like an autumn leaf, carried him 30 yards and deposited him in the hedge. As he struggled to regain his feet a huge stone from the embankment around the bombed tank smashed into the middle of his back. By contrast my grandfather was untouched, unhurt. He heard the bang, saw Freddie flying through the air and quickly made his way to his brother's side. 'They've got me, Ron,' gasped Freddie, drama queen to the last. 'I'm done for. Leave me, save yourself.'

Despite the dramatics, Freddie wasn't seriously injured, just winded. He lived to fight many other days and to enjoy his fame as a war casualty.

He wasn't the only connection between my family and that oil tank fire. The flames spread, slowly but surely, from one oil tank to the next until, in the end, eleven of them were ablaze. It was, at that time, the largest fire in Britain since the Great Fire of London in 1666, nearly 300 years before. Of course, there were bigger fires later in the war but for two weeks in August 1940 it seemed as if the whole of Pembroke Dock was likely to be consumed.

The Pembroke Dock Fire Chief, Arthur Morris, was yet another uncle of mine. He was married to Lizzie, Ronnie and Freddie's sister, and for the next two weeks, as the fire raged, he spent the whole time at the scene of the disaster. He never went to bed, but slept alongside the town's old Merryweather Fire Engine, exhausted and in real danger of incineration at any minute.

Firemen came from all over the country to help. Tragedy struck when the wall of one blazing tank ruptured and five Cardiff firemen were instantly consumed by the sheet

The oil tank fire of August 1940 was, at that time, the largest fire Britain had seen since the Great Fire of London in 1666. This photograph shows the huge cloud of smoke and oil that hung above the town for two solid weeks.

The only oil tank to survive, shown here in a photograph taken from the Barrack Hill in the 1980s before it was demolished to make way for a new nine holes and clubhouse for the town golf club.

of fire. Even in the early stages, it was clear that the firemen were facing a deadly and, ultimately, hopeless fight.

Oil poured from the damaged tanks, running in a raging river down Military Road, but my uncle Arthur and his men stuck to their task. Coated in oil, half-choked by the smoke and fumes that hung like a modern sword of Damocles above the town, they battled on, knowing they had to keep the fire in check. The whole of Pembroke Dock depended on their efforts.

Uncle Arthur was the stuff of which heroes are made, but when the awards, citations and medals were given out after the blaze had been finally quelled, he was totally overlooked. In contrast, one fireman who had spent only a few hours at the fire received the George Medal. It was never clear how or why the authorities arrived at their decision, but it caused a controversy in Pembroke Dock. Even now, it is one that still occasionally rears its ugly head.

As for the immediate family, we all lived together in that wonderful old house, which remains an essential and integral part of childhood memories. My father, mother and grandfather – Grampy Phillips as we all knew him. I don't really remember his wife that much, my maternal grandmother, as she died when I was four or five. They were the bedrock of the group. Then came me and, of course, trailing in my wake, my two sisters.

Anne arrived in the Queen's Coronation year, 1953; my youngest sister Judith in 1958. I suppose they were just that little bit too young to be playmates – I only know they were usually a damned nuisance, Anne standing on my Britain's lead soldiers, Judith putting scratches across my precious vinyl 45 records. It didn't stop me loving them, but playmates – no way!

Relatives apart, some of my earliest memories are concerned with animals.

First there was our cat, a large tabby creature we called Tibs or Tibby. He was an old farm cat who, in the main, shunned human contact until it was time for food. The one exception was my sister Anne. She could do anything with that creature and, once she got round to walking, the cat seemed to spend half of his life wrapped up like a baby, lying in her dolls pram. The looks he threw me as Anne wheeled him past left me in no doubt; he had found the good life. Until, one day, Anne decided to test the theory that cats, when they fell, always landed on their feet. She took Tibs to the top landing of the house and I saw in her eyes what she intended to do. Desperately I tried to grab the cat as she held it out over the banisters and let go.

Anne might have let go, the cat certainly didn't. I still sport a pair of wide tramline marks on my left forearm where his claws dug in and slid from elbow to wrist as he fell. It's true; cats do fall on their feet, even if this one then proceeded to bounce a further 6 feet along the hallway. He bore Anne no ill will. Next day, Tibs was back in her dolls pram, happily looking at the world through a pair of grey feline eyes as if the incident had never occurred.

The other animals of note were pigs. By the time I was four or five the family no longer farmed but Uncle Freddie still kept the yard – I don't really know why – and Grandfather held on to a pair of enormous pigs. They lived in a sty at the bottom of our long garden. Those pigs were his pride and joy, but I hated them with a vengeance I could barely place.

I used to lean on the corrugated iron wall of the sty, balancing myself on one of the stone pig troughs, and try to stare them out. The pigs shuffled and snuffled around in the mud

Above left: The dreaded Tibby – held, for once,
by yours truly – in the mid-1950s. The cat might be firmly held but he does not look happy.

Above right: Sisters and cousin. My sister Anne, back right, Judith in front, and cousin Chris on
the left in a photograph taken at a chapel Christmas party.

Uncle Arthur, hero of the blaze, sits on the right of the group in this family photograph. My
grandfather, Ron Phillips, is in the centre and another relative, Jack Ross – husband of Aunty
Della – is on the left. Behind them is the huge expanse of the Barrack Hill.

and muck. They were always haughty and arrogant, those pigs, and glared back with such malevolent eyes that it wasn't long before I beat a hasty retreat back up the garden path.

Of course, with food rationing still in place, the pigs were being carefully fattened until the time they could provide the family with bacon and pork. Perhaps, if I'd known about their short life expectancy, I'd have been a little more understanding. Then again, maybe not.

When the day came for the pigs to be transported to the slaughterhouse, I was warned to stay well out of the way. Dad, on the other hand, was press-ganged into helping out.

'I'll get the van doors open,' said Grandfather, ever the general. 'You get them out of the sty. Remember, hold onto their ears – it's the only grip you'll ever get.'

Dad had never worked with animals in all his life. He was a teacher, an artist. Pigs were not only alien to him; he hated them worse than I did.

'Don't forget – the ears!' Grandfather called, throwing open the van doors. Of course, the inevitable happened. Dad grabbed the first pig by the shoulder and tried to manoeuvre it out of the sty. The pig took off, Dad attached to its back and looking for the entire world like a Wild West bronco rider – straight through the fence and hedge of the adjoining garden.

It took hours to get the pig back and years later the shape of their passing, man and beast, still remained, cut into the hedge like one of those shapes you used to see in cartoon films.

We never had dogs, at least not until I was much older. Then my sister Anne managed to acquire a beautiful black Labrador. We called him Bond, after Ian Fleming's spy hero, but for some reason he also answered to the name Henry – or even, on occasions, Henry Bond.

Another family pet. This shows my sister Judith and the big black Labrador we called Bond, in the garden at No. 41.

Bond loved to play rough-and-tumble with me. I used to keep an old glove in the kitchen drawer. The minute I put it on – the minute I even went close to the drawer, come to that – he would dive for me and we would roll around the floor, Bond gnawing and clawing at my protected hand. The moment I said 'I give in, you win' he would stop and step back, knowing he had been triumphant yet again. I often wondered what would have happened if one of my aunts had appeared in the house, wearing their delicate lace gloves. It never happened.

Bond was nothing if not true to his name, a real ladies' man. He disappeared one day and dad decided that, as he was off 'on the razzle', as he put it, we ought to go and get him back. We searched everywhere – no sign of Bond. Then, outside St John's Church in town, we saw him sitting, exhausted and forlorn.

Dad pulled the car to a halt alongside him. Bond hung his head in shame – and exhaustion, I suppose.

'Get in,' dad ordered.

I opened the back door and the dog slunk in. When we got back to No. 41 we were astounded to see Bond – the real Bond – sitting on the doorstep. The two dogs were identical. We took the impostor back to town and he sidled morosely out of the car, as if knowing he had been found out.

And then, of course, there were the cows. They used to pass up and down our road every morning and evening, regular as clockwork and rarely attended by any human, on their way to and from Kenny Scourfield's farm and fields. They seemed to know exactly when and how to make the journey out and back. We didn't think anything of what I now see as a natural homing instinct, the cows were just there, doing what came naturally.

Cow pats down the centre of the road were commonplace. They lay there, steaming, in the wake of the herd, sometimes shovelled up to use in people's gardens but mostly just left there to wash away in the rain. Years later, my father, with something akin to relish, used to deliberately drive over these lumps of manure. He even made me do it when I started driving in the late 1960s. 'Good protection for the bottom of the car,' he would say. 'Stops the metal rotting.'

Then, as now, his logic escaped me – the car might stink but it would never rust away!

Pembroke Dock was a wonderful blend of urban and rural environments. This shows cows grazing peacefully on the Barrack Hill, not even bothering to look at the town laid out below them.

Chapter Two

New School, New Friends

I suppose everyone remembers at least a part of their first day at school. For me it was the row of crying newcomers, all standing there in their shorts and jumpers – pristine, new, bought for the occasion – tears pumping out of their eyes like water from an artesian well. There was no acclimatisation or slow introduction in those less cosseting and accommodating times. Deep-end philosophy was the order of the day. You turned up on the first day of term and just got on with it.

I can't honestly say that I was upset by the process of starting school as my father was a teacher. I knew he was human and didn't eat young children. He came home at lunchtime and in the evening, so the day held no terror for me.

I suppose, with hindsight, starting school marked the end of one stage of my life. At the time the thought never crossed my mind and it did, after all, open up a brand-new world of experience and friendship.

The school – Pennar Junior Mixed – was an old board school and, like all Victorian school buildings, was made up of thick walls and windows set so high that even the teachers had difficulty looking out. There was certainly no chance of anything taking place outside distracting the pupils, teachers or visitors contained within its walls.

The school was a singularly unattractive building. The inside walls were painted a dull green, desks were aligned in perfect order and the lights seemed to be burning all day long. In the winter, heating was provided by one coal burning stove at the front of each classroom; its heat barely reached 3 feet and as this was the spot where teachers invariably stood to warm their backsides; they basked in an eternal summer while the class shivered and froze.

The playground in front of the school was sloping and bounded by high stone walls. These days it would probably be regarded as a Health and Safety hazard. We seemed to spend all of our play and lunchtimes striding around this area in a long row, arms linked and chanting, 'Who wants a game of cowboys and Indians?' If anyone did, they simply joined on the end of the line. Strangely, while I can remember the recruiting process I have no memory of any game ever being started.

The back playground, between the infants and junior departments, was a drab, uninteresting place – apart from the large and pristine climbing-frame that stood there. We lived under express instructions never to go near the gleaming bars and framework. In fact, not once in all the years I attended the school did I see anyone ever use or climb on the thing. We would have loved to clamber over it and swing from the contraption and I still wonder what it was doing there, apart from teasing and admonishing all the pupils. Perhaps it was meant to be a lesson in self-control!

Across the road stood the school hall, actually part of St Patrick's Church and used in the evenings by the local cubs and scout groups. Almost alongside this long, low building was Pennar Park. It was just a field, really, with some swings and a seesaw at the top end but it was here that, every year, we held our school sports day.

The swings, of course, were a great draw. We used to regale each other with the tale of one boy who had swung so high he'd gone right over the top and killed himself by falling onto the concrete base the Council had so conveniently put in beneath the swings. None of us knew his name, naturally enough, but everyone swore the story was true.

There were always compensations for any hardships we endured. Pennar School was where I first met the friends who were to become constants in my life. Bob Howells and Kenny Deveson lived close by, in Lower Pennar and Bufferland respectively, while Stephan Shamrock's house lay just two hundred yards away down Military Road. We sat together, played together, grew to adolescence together. Now it is still impossible to think of the school without images of those three friends crowding into my brain.

Before school my friendships had been centred on the family, on uncles, aunts and my cousins Ken and Christine, but school suddenly and irrevocably broadened my horizons, all our horizons I suppose, and things could never be the same again.

The images of those days proliferate. In particular, there is Mrs Rees. She taught what was known as the 'Scholarship Class', in effect cramming us in English, maths and something euphemistically called intelligence in order that we might pass the dreaded 11-plus examination and so get into Pembroke Grammar School.

If ever there was a wilful and destructive misinterpretation of government legislation it has to be the 11-plus, or scholarship, exam. The 1944 Education Act had established three types of secondary school – grammar, secondary modern and technical. The system was supposed to give each child the education to which they were best suited.

What happened, of course, was that parents – and teachers – immediately saw the Grammar School option as the top, the best, and academically minded children were duly streamed off and coached in order to pass the exam. Even those who were never going to go within a mile of Grammar School were forced to endure the process. It didn't matter what you wanted out of life; that was irrelevant.

Thousands of children had their education, even their childhoods, destroyed by this cramming, by the relentless ambition of parents - and by teachers, who measured their success by the number of 'passes' from their class and school. The mark of failure hung around the necks of those who didn't quite make the grade, scarring them for life.

My cousin Ken and I waiting patiently on the quay at Tenby while the White Funnel paddler behind us begins to take on passengers. To the right of this image, Pennar School is visible.

A group of children and young people from Lower Pennar at a street party for the Coronation of Queen Elizabeth. My friend Bob Howells, clad in shirt and tie, sits at the extreme-right end of the second row up.

Mrs Rees offered a limited curriculum with very little history or geography, next to no PE or science and certainly no foreign languages, but she did have a unique way of making her point.

I was probably eight or nine when I first saw her at work. One of my classmates, a boy called Calvin Payne, whiled away one boring afternoon of maths and more maths by inscribing his name across and around a large piece of blotting paper. 'Calvin Payne is a very good boy,' it read. As a piece of calligraphy it was beautifully done, but Mrs Rees took exception.

'Waste!' she screamed. 'Waste, waste, waste! How dare you?'

Poor Calvin was dragged out to the front of the class and his never-to-be-forgotten phrase – 'Calvin Payne is a very good boy' – was slapped out in perfect time on the bare flesh of his left thigh. I don't remember how Calvin took his beating, but I do remember the glazed look in Mrs Rees' eyes and the spittle on her lips as she struck down, again and again and again. I don't suppose it mattered too much but it was Calvin's own ink and blotting paper.

Years later I wrote a poem about this tyrant who ruled our lives and our every thought for two or three years. She was autocratic, undoubtedly had her favourites and was quite brutal in her teaching methods, but she was 'of her time' and whatever else I thought of her, she did certainly give us all a fine grounding in the basics of English grammar. I think I'm grateful:-

Old Mrs Rees was vicious.
When Mrs Rees got mad,
She'd spit and shout, she'd call you "Lout!"
Duw, Mrs Rees was bad.
Mrs Rees taught English, Maths,
The only things she knew,

Left History and CDT
For someone else to do.

When Mrs Rees taught spelling,
She'd slap out every word
Upon your leg, until you'd beg –
A plea she never heard.

Mrs Rees had favourites,
They'd gather round her knee.
We'd watch and hate, they'd sit in state,
Where we all longed to be.

Then Mrs Rees said "Listen
To what I'm going to say.
This hurts me more than you, I'm sure
You'll thank me one fine day.

I only ever wanted
To see you all get on.
You must feel free to visit me –
You'll miss me when I'm gone."

Then Mrs Rees retired,
Gave up her class and cane.
She sat at home, old and alone –
And no-one ever came.

The last verse is more imagination than reality – a little revenge, perhaps? I suppose, these days, Mrs Rees wouldn't have lasted two minutes in a classroom but, in those far off, post-war days, corporal punishment was the norm.

My generation at primary school in the 1950s endured the last vestiges of the old British Empire. Bob and I would sit, half listening, as Mrs Rees or, more usually, one of the other teachers, specifically dragooned in for the lesson, ranted on about Scott of the Antarctic or Drake's Drum; anything that would extol British supremacy and the virtues of fair play.

I suppose it was one of the results of the war, so recently fought and won, but in those days anything British was noble and to be admired. The Union Jack seemed always to be flying above our heads, fluttering and flapping in the winds of the Imperial retreat.

It was the time of the Mau Mau in Africa, the Malayan emergency and Archbishop Makarios in Cyprus. At the time we instinctively supported Britain in these conflicts. The thought that people were fighting for their freedom never entered our brainwashed heads. Only much later did the beginnings of realisation dawn on us.

And so, at the time, we applauded and basked in reflected glory when Hilary and Tensing, members of the British-led expedition under Sir John Hunt, became the first men to climb Mount Everest. We avidly followed the exploits of Malcolm Campbell as he strove to break the world land and water speed records.

Stirling Moss, Stanley Matthews and Cliff Morgan were our heroes and we scoured the newspapers for reports of cricket matches when famous names like Len Hutton, Peter May and Godfrey Evans ruled the county cricket scene. When they took the fight for the Ashes to the mighty Australians we waited avidly for news of the results, nails bitten to the quick.

I suppose it was inevitable that we played at war. All children did in those days. We would roar through a patch of undergrowth and bushes, known as the School Gardens, which lay between my house and the back entry to our school, firing make-believe rifles and machine guns. In my memory the area was huge, full of hidden grottoes. In reality, of course, it was barely 100 yards, top to bottom.

Then there was the Barrack Hill. It was a large plateau of grass, effectively the top of the ridge that separated Pennar from Pembroke Dock. At the eastern end was the huge bulk of the Defensible Barracks, originally built to house the soldiers who defended the dockyard, while to the west stood the village of Llanreath.

The hill itself might be open and relatively flat, boasting both a soccer pitch and a concrete cricket strip – you were supposed to lay coconut matting on top but we never did – but its flanks were covered by thickets of gorse, brambles and trees of an indeterminate and ill-defined nature. This was where we loved to roam and play.

On the southern slope lay an old stone bridge, carrying a walkway across a thickly wooded gully and a stream that, eventually, fell down the hill through Llanreath and exited as a mere trickle into Milford Haven. It might have been small but, to us, it was as big as the Amazon or the Mississippi and to follow the stream all the way from its source to its 'eruption' into the Haven was every bit as exciting as Livingstone or Burton trying to find the source of the Nile.

Sometimes we would roam across the Barrack Hill – less than half a mile from my front door – and its flanking woods, flitting like shadows between the trees, setting ambushes and screaming like dervishes as the enemy – either imaginary or boys from Llanreath or Bufferland – walked, unsuspecting, into our trap.

At other times we played as cowboys instead of soldiers, but that variation was dependent on which film we'd recently seen at Haggar's or the Grand, the two cinemas available to us. After sitting, enthralled, through *The Magnificent Seven*, we played 'cowboys' for weeks on end. None of us wanted to be Yul Brynner or any of the others who were killed off one by one as the film progressed, but overnight Steve McQueen became our hero. In the years to come we loyally watched every film he ever made.

What we really enjoyed, and what we did best, was digging trenches. My garden was long and narrow, bordered by the dairy from the old farm at the top, the pigsty at the bottom. In between stood grandfather's enormous tin shed where he botched around and carried out repairs. The garden was a wonderland, the perfect place to dig row after row of trenches and recreate our version of the Western Front.

We were probably seven or eight when we first tried it. By the time we were ten we had the digging and the layout down to a fine art. Every summer a network of trenches would coil like an intestine across and around the garden – front line, communication trenches and, once, even a dugout, complete with a roof built of stakes from Uncle Freddie's farmyard.

Edmund Hilary on the summit of Mount Everest. We revelled in the success of this New Zealander – but the expedition to conquer the world's highest mountain was, at least, led by a Briton.

Stanley Matthews, one of our idols, was a household name in the 1950s – and to think he did it all with a ball that was like a piece of concrete.

Above left: The huge and imposing Defensible Barracks on the eastern end of the Barrack Hill. It was supposedly built in just twelve months – if that is true it must rank as one of the most incredible feats of engineering and construction ever accomplished.

Above right: Bufferland, like Pennar and Llanreath, was another tiny suburb above the town, a distinct community which prided itself on its independence.

The village of Llanreath at the western end of the Barrack Hill, notable for its steep hill down to the beach – great when going down, a devil when climbing back up.

We were careful and I, for one, was always a little wary about sitting there in that subterranean hollow, the earth groaning and creaking above my head. I certainly didn't fancy 10 tons of earth collapsing on top of me. In the event the roof never did give way but there was near disaster one year when Bob, hammering at the trench floor with a pick axe, suddenly saw the ground open up beneath his feet.

He leapt for safety as soft brown earth poured through the ever-widening gap in the ground. The smell that began to escape from the hole was putrid and foul.

'Get my grandfather, quick!' I shouted, trying hard to claw my way out of what was now clearly a dangerous location.

When Grandfather appeared, braces around his waist and the remains of a Woodbine stuck onto his lower lip, he took one look and ushered us away. 'Get away,' he declared. 'That's the old cess pit for the house. It goes down twenty feet.'

'Cess pit?' I asked. 'What's a cess pit?' My mate Kenny, always knowledgeable about things like that, nudged me in the ribs. 'From the days before they had flush toilets, you dim wit. That's what's making the stink.' I punched him, he punched me back and we wrestled as Grandfather fetched two planks from the old dairy and laid them over the hole. Then he carefully covered the area with earth before going back to his newspaper and the radio. 'Don't play here,' he called, over his shoulder. 'Dig somewhere else.'

Of course, we waited until his broad back disappeared into the house and then carried on, exactly as before.

Our trench digging finally came to an end after we persuaded my father to play a part in our game. We needed an enemy, someone to attack us in our trenches, and dad was always happy to indulge us in our whims. We left the house with his warning ringing in our ears. He would attack at 8.00 p.m. that evening.

We lay in the trenches and waited as the day slowly died. We knew he was coming, but when, suddenly, a water bomb – a plastic bag filled with water – burst on the parapet in front of me, it took us all by surprise.

'Run!' I shrieked and we took to our heels, heading for the security of the old pigsty. Dad, already knowing he had won the battle, hurled more water bombs which fell on our heads and backs as we ran. Then he leapt onto the top of the large stone wall that bordered the garden and raised his arms in triumph. 'Victory!' he shouted. 'Victory is mine!'

At that moment, my cousin Ken hurled one of the few weapons we possessed. It was an old and rotting onion, plucked from the dark recesses of the dairy. Ken's throw was unerringly accurate. Down the garden it flew, directly towards Dad. It hit him squarely in the eye, the squashed and dissolving onion rings disintegrating and spreading like sea spray around his head.

Needless to say, that was the end of the exercise – and our game. My friends were sent packing and I was despatched to bed while dad lay, moaning, in the lounge with a piece of steak on his throbbing, blackened eye. 'What do you expect?' I heard grandfather say as I closed the living room door on the scene. 'Grown man acting like a bloody child!'

No. 41 Military Road was a rambling old building with long, gloomy passageways, four rooms downstairs and six up above. There was a half-landing at the top of the first flight of stairs and shadows, dark and mysterious shadows, always seemed to linger and lurk around the landing corners.

The stairs were steep with a beautiful oak balustrade or set of banisters, ideal for sliding down. The trick was to see how far I could fly through the air once I reached the bottom of the run.

A huge glass door, made up of small coloured glass panels, guarded the front lobby and this was the target, but it lay a good 15 feet from the bottom of the stairs and I never quite managed to reach it. Perhaps it was just as well as I'd have undoubtedly cut my hands to ribbons if they'd ever smashed up against that lobby door.

Climbing the stairs, from outside the banisters, was another pasttime. The first section caused no problem but switching to the upper set of railings was both difficult and dangerous. It involved swinging around, letting go with one hand and grabbing for the banister poles with the other – all in one movement. I never fell but when I think about what would have happened if I had, well, it makes my skin crawl.

My friends and I were always climbers. We started on the toilet roof – no indoor loo in those days – shinnying up in order to jump like parachutists onto the soft dark earth of grandfather's vegetable patch. Bob, Kenny, Stephan, all the others, we all made the jump, although not when anyone was inside the toilet!

When that grew too tame we turned our attention to grandfather's shed, clambering up from the toilet onto the sloping tin roof. The fact that the corrugated iron was old and rusted made no difference. We didn't think what might have happened to our flesh had the roof given way and we had fallen through into the darkness beneath.

Grandfather had the shed pulled down when I was eight or nine – it had become far too dilapidated – and, always eager to extend our horizons, we began to think about No. 41 itself. It was a tall building, 50 foot if it was an inch, with a long extension running out from the back wall. We quickly realised that if we dropped the sash window of my bedroom we could climb out onto the ledge and reach for the guttering of the extension.

From that exposed and precarious position we were able to shimmy up the tiles of the extension – lethal when it was raining but always a lot more fun – to sit astride the apex of the building and gaze out over the fields. From there you could see right over Pembroke River to the South Pembrokeshire peninsula and, if you shuffled far enough forward, there was even a view of far-off Pembroke Castle.

Coming down was a tricky business as you had to slide down the tiles, jam your feet into the guttering as a brake and dive – perhaps fall might be a better description – for the open window on the adjoining wall. Miss the guttering and it was a 50-foot nosedive onto the concrete of the back yard but the danger never once entered our heads.

That was another game that came to an untimely end when my mother, coming back from hanging out washing, happened to glance up and see me perched on the top of the house. She screamed and I jumped so high, so far, that I nearly lost my balance and joined her down below. Mum called for Dad and once again Bob and the rest were sent home while my backside was sore for a week afterwards.

The sash windows of my bedroom were a real boon for us. We flew our model aeroplanes from there, standing on the wide inner ledge and despatching them down the garden. The planes were small, balsa wood models that we glued together and were powered by an elastic band attached to the propeller. You wound the propeller, thus tightening the band and, when you thought you had enough power, you simply let them go.

My sister Anne on the swing in our back garden. The swing stood where Grampy Phillips' old shed had once been. On the left of the photograph is the outside toilet where we began our climbing activities.

Dad, Mum, Anne and me in the back yard of No. 41. Look at the height of the houses – to think we really did climb onto the roof of the building!

The planes were amateurish and hand-made, a bit like the flying machines of the Great War, but making them take to the air was as exciting as any 'Biggles' book we had ever read. Sometimes those planes even made it to the bottom of the garden. The only exception was Kenny Deveson. Always single-minded, he announced one day that he was going to fly jets for the RAF – he did, in due course becoming a Vulcan bomber pilot – and that our elastic-band planes were things of the past.

Kenny bought himself a model jet. He spent hours on the plane, sanding the wings, fiddling with the jet engine. On launch day he stood on the window ledge, ignited the engine and we all watched as, with a roar you could have heard in nearby Pembroke, the machine hurtled into the air. It was last seen disappearing in the direction of Pembroke River, half a mile to the south.

The window did, occasionally, cause problems, however. Bob always had a good throwing arm and one day, after an immense wind up of arm and body, he hurled out his plane. This was going to be the flight to beat all flights, we thought, knowing that the long distance record set two or three months before was under serious threat.

Unfortunately for Bob, his momentum took him forward and his head smashed against the top of the window frame. His knees shot out – straight through two panes of glass. 'Windows Howells,' my father promptly christened him. It was a name that stuck for years, even after Bob and I had grown to manhood and Dad was in his dotage. 'Here comes Windows Howells,' he would sing out whenever Bob hove into view. 'Call the glazier!'

A fly-past of Sunderlands, watched by people from Llanreath and Pennar.

How the papers envisaged it – a patriotic publicity view of life at home in the 1940s and '50s. In fact, in Pennar, we had no electricity until the 1950s were well advanced and gas mantles, while atmospheric, gave nowhere near as much light as this.

Bob and I had many narrow escapes during those early childhood years. So many, in fact, that I often wonder how either of us ever made it to adulthood.

I still remember Bob showing me how to ricochet air gun pellets off the ground. The pellets shot away down our garden path with a beautifully satisfying whine. It was unfortunate that Uncle Freddie from next door was leaning against the line post some 20 yards down the garden. The first pellet shot between his hand and his head, the second one clipped the bottom of his ear. He chased us for miles, showing an incredible turn of speed for a man of his age, all the while holding a handkerchief to his bleeding ear.

That air gun of Bob's must have been jinxed. Once we were engaged in a little target practice in his garden and, working to the age-old premise that if you aim at something you will never hit it, he drew a careful bead on the stalk of one of his father's prized daffodils. It was the shot of the year and slowly, ever so slowly, the top of the flower rocked, slid to the side and fell.

We found some sellotape in the kitchen drawer and hurriedly taped the yellow head – still hanging by the slimmest of threads – back in place. Then I headed for home and

Bob carefully concealed the gun in the shed. He must have got away with it – at least or a while – because I cannot recall any retribution from his father descending on me.

We played with air guns and bows and arrows that we made from sticks found in the woods. Bob quickly became an expert with the throwing spear. He would cut and shave the straightest stick he could find and then wrap string around the end. When he threw the missile, using the string to provide extra whip, it went off like a shot from a sling, lancing through the air towards its target. My efforts barely managed 10 feet. Bob later put his skill to great use when we moved on to the Grammar School, becoming the school javelin champion and setting a record that remains unbroken, even to this day.

We were made to feel at home in all of the houses where friends and relatives lived. Bob and his family moved from Lower Pennar into a new council house in Cross Park when I was seven or eight. It was on a direct route up to the Barrack Hill and so both of us were happy with the arrangement. Kenny and Stephan lived in smaller houses so it was always easier to congregate at my house where there was the garden to utilise and plenty of empty rooms to occupy us on wet days.

No. 41, like all of the other houses in our street, was lit by gas light and candles, at least until I was about seven or eight. Electricity was simply not supplied to Pennar until the early 1950s and until that great and glorious day when it was finally laid on, ours was a world of guttering gas mantles and shadows that seemed to dance like sunbeams across the walls.

It was a comforting and comfortable world, those gas-lit days of early childhood. Sitting in front of a roaring log fire with a book on my lap – *Treasure Island*, *The Hound of the Baskervilles* or the latest *Biggles* tome – and the radio playing, and the gas lamps guttering and spluttering behind my head, there was nowhere in the world I would rather have been.

I'd be the last person to say that the gas light was efficient. Apart from anything else I seemed to spend half my life running down the road to the shop to buy gas mantles! But gas light was certainly atmospheric. When they finally connected us up for electricity, some of the magic suddenly seemed to vanish from childhood.

Chapter Three
Entertainment

Our entertainment in the '50s was quite limited, certainly when compared to what is available to children and young people in the twenty-first century. We didn't have a television – well, there was no electricity so there would have been no point – but we did have the radio; the wireless as it was then called.

It was provided by what we called 'the relay'. As far as I have been able to find out, this was a wireless network, a sort of early cable channel, provided by a shop in town. It only gave us the Home and Light Programmes and even after the arrival of electricity my parents insisted on keeping it, much to my annoyance.

Uncle Jim and Aunty Ave, just down the road, had a radiogram and they were able to tune in, among other things, to Radio Luxembourg. I would sit with my cousin Ken some evenings and listen to the serials they broadcast – *Riders of the Range* and *PC 49* amongst others. Back home I would have to entertain myself with organ music or *Brain of Britain*, but then came *Journey into Space*. It used to be broadcast in the evenings at 7.00 p.m., just before my bedtime. It was a serial adventure telling the story of intrepid space travellers and all the alien worlds they encountered. I don't remember much about the actual programme, just the echoing voice at the beginning and the fact that Alfie Bass played one of the travellers.

After *Journey into Space* it was time for bed. I used to traipse up the stairs with my candle, terrified at every creak of the stairs, every rush of wind outside the windows. I would then make my poor father stand at the bottom of the stairs and sing or recite poetry to me until I dropped off to sleep.

For some reason I can still remember one particular poem he used to spout, although its title and the author have long been forgotten. It went something like this:-

    Up the airy mountain,
    Down the rushy glen,
    We dare not go a'hunting
    For fear of little men.

If it wasn't that one, it was verses by someone like Rudyard Kipling or Sir Henry Newbolt. The sentiments of the poems, even their subjects, meant little to me. It was the strong rolling rhythms and the cadences that I loved.

Dad's voice was nothing special, but it didn't stop me enjoying the evening concert! Usually, for some reason, it was hymns; 'Onward Christian Soldiers' – that type of thing, but no matter how scared I was, nothing would ever induce me to miss an episode of *Journey into Space*.

In the garden at No. 41. Left to right: Mum, my cousin Ken, me. My sister Anne is in front. Notice the same knitted cardigans on Ken and I – almost compulsory in those days. The only difference seems to be in the sailors' hat I am wearing.

Cowboy films were hugely popular in the 1950s. They provided a degree of glamour in what was, otherwise, quite a hard world. This advertising poster is for the unlamented and long-forgotten *Battle of Rogue River*.

John Wayne – shown here, for once, out of cowboy attire.

There were other programmes of note. *Hancock's Half Hour* and *The Goon Show* were two I particularly remember. Tony Hancock's lugubrious voice and the sheer idiocy of Kenneth Williams were a joy to anyone's ears.

Later came *Round the Horn* and *The Navy Lark* – Lesley Phillips with his 'Left hand down a bit' could have been me navigating a rowing boat on the Mill Pond in Pembroke. The power of words, even then, impinged itself on my mind, far more lasting and certainly more effective than any visual image.

Mind you, the cinema was still an important part of childhood. First there was the Saturday Morning Matinee, just for us youngsters. Every weekend we settled ourselves into the plush seats of the Grand Cinema and hoped against hope that, this week, the projector would not break down.

The Grand was just a tin shack with a brick-built entrance and when it rained they had to turn up the volume so that you could actually hear what was being said on the screen over the sound of rain on the corrugated iron roof. It hardly mattered to most of the kids; they were more intent on throwing sweet papers at each other, but for me, that silver screen opened up a whole world of adventure.

On those magical Saturday mornings I sailed the Seven Seas with Sinbad, explored jungles with Tarzan and even flew through the air with Superman – 'Up, up and away,' as he used to shout. It didn't matter that the actor was decidedly overweight and paunchy; it was story-telling at its very best.

We had two cinemas available to us, Haggar's in Pembroke and The Grand in Pembroke Dock. Haggar's was run by descendants of the great William Haggar, one of the earliest pioneer film makers in Britain. They had turned to operating cinemas when William Haggar, a showman from the old days of bioscopes and travelling fairs, finally retired.

Years later I went to the local grammar school with two of the Haggar daughters, Susan and Dinah, but when I first began to sit in their cinema at the western end of Main Street in Pembroke, all that was light-years away.

Haggar's was a 'back to front' cinema, in other words you came in past the screen and made your way to your seat, glancing over your shoulder at flickering images in your rear. I must have lost count of the number of times I fell over someone's heels through trying to watch the old Pearl & Dean adverts that they showed at the beginning of every show.

An evening at the cinema was something to look forward to in the 1950s, people dressing up in their best clothes for the occasion and maybe even enjoying tea first at Brown's Café in Pembroke or Monti's in the 'Dock'. Then they (we, I should say) would sit through three hours of movies – a first feature, cartoons, newsreels and, finally, the big picture.

With family and friends, I watched everything and anything I could. Cowboys were always popular and hugely exotic – even if very rarely accurate. Hollywood's version of the Wild West story usually starred people like Jimmy Stewart, Burt Lancaster and, of course, John Wayne.

For a while the Davy Crockett story caught all our imaginations, Fess Parker's coonskin hat, complete with tail, spelling the demise of many old fur coats that would otherwise have lain unworn in the back of people's spare wardrobes.

One day I decided that my Davy Crockett outfit was desperately in need of a powder flask – a cow horn to everyone else – and my cousin Ken and I duly visited the local slaughterhouse. They were very obliging and gave us two horns each, blood and flesh still attached. When I presented them to my mother and asked her if she could clean them out, we had more screams and my prized possessions were consigned to the dustbin. I never did get my powder horns.

Both the Grand and Haggar's were independent cinemas – the days of the big chains being some way in the future – so we had to wait for new releases, sometimes for months. I remember mum declaring that she would have to go to Swansea or Cardiff – no mean trip, either of them, in those days – if *South Pacific* didn't come to Pembroke Dock pretty soon.

The Grand was a wonderful place. There was a small shop where you could buy things like ice cream and chocolate but there was no toilet. If you wanted to visit the loo during the evening you had to run across the road to the town public toilets. That was fine if the weather was good, not so pleasant if it was raining.

Sitting there in the darkness with columns of cigarette smoke snaking up through the light beams from the projector, I felt safe and happy, like a king, a witness to stories and tales that nobody else had ever encountered before. Glancing over my shoulder into the darkness of the back rows I could dimly make out coiled shapes and figures, but, at seven or eight years old, I had no idea what was going on back there. That would come later.

When television finally arrived in Pembroke Dock and Pennar, courtesy of the new electricity supply, it gradually killed off the power and the enjoyment of the cinema.

My Uncle Arthur (he of oil tank fame) and Aunty Lizzie were the first people in our street to actually own a set, a tiny grey device set inside a wooden box. You could hardly see what was happening for zigzag lines across the screen and if, by some miracle, interference was absent, you had to be within 6 feet of the box to pick out individual characters.

Nevertheless, in 1953 we duly crowded around the set to watch the Coronation of our new queen, still clutching the commemorative mugs and propelling pencils we had been given in school and at the chapel tea parties. Afterwards, in the weeks and months to come, we would crowd into Aunt Lizzie's lounge each evening at five o' clock to watch the latest episode of *The Cisco Kid* or *The Range Rider*.

Chapel, of course, was a central and essential part of our lives. Grandfather was a deacon and sang bass in the choir of Gilgal Baptist chapel and so, for my sisters and I, there was no choice. We would attend.

Having said that, I loved the old chapel, not for any particular religious connotations it might have but because of the whole atmosphere and ambience of the place, its white-walled simplicity and the deep, dark, swirling oak patterns on the pulpit and pews. There was serenity about the place that was totally appealing. The building was always so cool and comforting. 'God's breath,' my grandfather used to smile. I didn't know about that, but if God had to be somewhere, surely there was no better place for him to live?

By contrast, I hated the white-washed Sunday School room. The moment I entered the place I knew it smacked of oppression and indoctrination – and quite apart from anything else, we had to go to school five days a week, why inflict more discipline and order onto us every Sunday afternoon?

In the week, of course, it was different. The list of chapel activities seemed to be endless – among others there were Band of Hope, Youth Club, Drama Group and the inevitable series of rehearsals for the Sunday School Anniversary. I don't know what anniversary we were preparing for but we seemed to do it every year. Each year Bob, Stephan and I – not Kenny Deveson, he went to Bethany chapel in Bufferland – would carefully and progressively carry out and build up models of the chapel, a church, a lighthouse (to show the light, of course), each one of us reciting a poem or a piece of prose before adding our piece to the 3D jigsaw. I still remember, to my eternal chagrin, trying to give a passable rendition of Robbie Burns's 'A Man's a Man for a' that' in a highly dubious Scottish accent. My father must have died from shame.

All winter we used the chapel as a base for evening activities, mingling with friends from school, shouting and laughing and barely giving a thought to what the chapel was really all about. Then, at the end of the evening, it was home, past the yellow glow of the chip shop in Nelson Street – a yellow glow, which, along with the fumes and fragrances, always drew us in.

After the chip shop came the long walk up a pitch-dark lane, glancing back over our shoulders and dreading the vampires and demons that lurked in the shadows. Panic usually set in for the last 20 or so yards and we would flee, racing for our lives, desperate to reach the security of the yellow lamp-lights in Military Road.

Cars were few in number, my father never owning such a thing until I was thirteen or fourteen. Uncle Jim had one but, then, he was a fitter and always seemed to have his head stuck under the bonnet of his prized Vauxhall Victor. Petrol was still rationed in the early 1950s and so we rarely ventured out in the gleaming car, but when we did go, it was always a trip to remember.

In the summer months we went on trips to the beach, to places like Freshwater West and, in particular, the safe and secluded bay at Angle. I always liked Freshwater West with its high dunes and long, open beach but the undertow at the water's edge was deadly and you swam there at your peril. Dozens of ships had been lost on the beach or the flanking cliffs over the years and, at low tide, you could still see the keel of one unlucky victim of the sea, sand and rocks. Mum decided, early on, that Angle was far safer. It was much smaller and more self-contained than 'Fresh West' as we called it. Perhaps that was part of its appeal.

Angle Bay, as far as mum was concerned, was one of the safest and best beaches in the whole of Pembrokeshire. Wide open to the Atlantic, Dad liked it because he could watch the ships beating into Milford Haven.

Cilcal Baptist Chapel, Pennar.

The beautiful sands of Freshwater West. There were two Freshwaters, West and East, but nowhere was the sand more inviting than Freshwater West.

Angle's wonderful strip of sand lay, perhaps, 15 miles away from home but Uncle Jim would make three or four trips to get the whole family out there. Then we'd settle down with sandwiches and a primus stove to brew tea as my father, dressed in sports jacket and flannels – his one concession to the day being to remove his tie – pointed out the ships making their way past West Angle Bay into the broad expanse of Milford Haven.

Dad was hugely knowledgeable about the ships, easily and quickly identifying the type and even, on occasions, giving us their names as well. As we watched and ate our sandwiches he would tell us stories about the Haven. It was from him that I heard the story of the Welsh Whisky Galore, an event that took place on and around Thorne Island, just a quarter of a mile off West Angle Bay.

In 1890 the schooner 'Loch Shiel', bound for Adelaide with a cargo of 100 per cent proof whisky, went ashore on the island and began to break up. The cargo floated inland, onto the beach at Angle, and the locals quickly realised what fate had thrown their way. Before the customs officers arrived they had spirited away crates of the stuff, some of the bottles being concealed down the legs of the women's bloomers.

Much of the contraband was hidden in the cottages at Angle, false walls being built in front of the bottles. Some of it was forgotten, only to re-appear years later when house improvements were being made in the village. Sadly, three people died trying to acquire the whisky, one of alcohol poisoning, the other two drowned when their rowing boat capsized in the waves.

Dad's tales were an important part of those days on the beach, but there was more, so much more. We'd play cricket on the sand and bathe in the sea. If the tide was in we'd dive and swim from the walls at the entrance to what we called the 'harbour', a small lagoon for the mooring of fishing boats and other craft. I could never persuade Dad to join us but Uncle Jim and aunts like Ave and Jean happily changed into bathing costumes and joined in the fun.

Then it was back to Pembroke Dock, Uncle Jim making his obligatory three trips, with my cousins Ken and Christine, my sisters and me always trying desperately to stay out of the way until the last journey in order to get an extra hour on the beach.

The harbour at Angle where, at high tide, we would swim and dive from the rocks on the left of the photograph.

AGL.43 Thorn Island, ANGLE

Thorn Island – sometimes spelled Thorne – was the scene of a famous shipwreck at the end of the nineteenth century. The old fort on top of the island was originally built to protect the dockyard 6 miles up the Haven. It never fired its guns in anger and was later converted into a hotel.

Poor Uncle Jim; those journeys must have seemed endless. By the time of the third trip home petrol would be running low and I can clearly recall Jim switching off the ignition whenever we ran down a steep hill then bump starting the car when we reached the bottom.

Occasionally, perhaps just once a year, we ventured further afield, to the 7-mile-long, rock-hard sands of Pendine on the Carmarthenshire–Pembrokeshire border. Attempts on the world land speed record had been held on those sands back in the early days of the twentieth century, Malcolm Campbell achieving a speed of 174.22 miles per hour to claim the record in February 1927.

In an attempt to better that, Welshman J. G. Parry-Thomas came to Pendine on 3 March the same year. Tragically, the drive chain of his car 'Babs' snapped and decapitated him. The car slewed out of control and crashed.

They buried the car somewhere on the beach, as a mark of respect, and no more attempts on the land speed record were made at Pendine. We all knew the story and often wondered where the remains of the car lay. One particular day I must have driven Dad crazy with requests to play cricket and, finally, in exasperation, he threw me a bucket and spade. 'Here,' he called, 'go and dig for "Babs". Half a mile that way!'

Ken and I spent hours digging in a futile attempt to uncover the car. We loved it and, strangely, searching for the car became something of a tradition in our family and the annual trip to Pendine was always eagerly anticipated. In 1969 a man from North Wales was given permission to excavate the car and now 'Babs', beautifully restored, goes on display at the local Museum of Speed every summer.

Car trips were a rarity and walking was the standard way of getting anywhere in those days. We'd walk to the shop, walk to town, walk to the nearest beach, if needs be.

Our trips into Pembroke Dock were the same every Saturday. Down the road and into Jack Howard's shop – Uncle Jack as we called him although he was no relative – for Dad to buy his Senior Service and a Mars bar or a packet of Smiths Crisps for my sister Anne and me. After that it was up to Bethany Corner with the town and the Haven spread-eagled down below us, down Tregenna's Hill and into the town itself. Our route never changed.

Dad would make his regular calls each Saturday. First we went Rees's Grocery Store, to drop off the order for the week's food. Then into Allen's toy shop for an hour's chat with Bill Grey. Bill ran the shop that had once been home to the premier photographer in the town, S. J. Allen. The Misses Allen were still there, terrible and daunting with their frosty frowns and grey powdered hair, tutting at me as I played with the toys, read all the books and quietly prepared my Christmas list.

From there it was down Bush and Meyrick Streets to Smith & Sons, a green-painted wonderland with its magazine and paperback book section wide open to the street. Half-way down Meyrick Street was Warren's Fish Shop, selling the best chips in town. The smell was exquisite, no matter how full you were. 'On the way back,' Dad would say.

Anne and I fell for it every time. When we made our way back up the street in an hour's time Warren's had invariably closed for the day. When we did find them open, the chips – sold in home-made cones so that the vinegar and tiny bits of crackling and potato always gathered in the bottom – were superb and the bits in the bottom of the cone were best of all. 'Mind you don't drink that vinegar,' Mum used to warn when we told her that we'd been to Warren's. 'It'll dry up your blood.' We never listened and the last time I took a look at my blood it seemed pretty liquid to me.

At least once a month Dad would take us on a trip across the Haven on one of the old ferry boats that operated from Hobbs Point. The ferries were tiny by today's standards, big enough for the occasional car but, in the main, catering largely for foot passengers.

Never mind their size, the *Alumchine* and *Lady Magdalene*, paddler and screw-driven vessels respectively, were like ocean liners to Anne and me. When, in time, they were replaced by the *Cleddau Queen* and *Cleddau King* the ferry boats still managed to retain their glamour and their appeal.

We would stand expectantly as one of the ferries, whichever one happened to be working that day, set off from the pontoon at Neyland across the river. The pontoon was situated directly below Brunel's old railway terminus, some of the old broad gauge rails now acting as a fence at the top of the walkway. Slowly but steadily the *Alumchine* or the *Cleddau King* would inch towards us and the excitement in our bellies would grow like a gathering thunderstorm until, at last, we could clamber on board and set off.

'Babs', the resurrected and re-vamped racing car of Parry-Thomas who was killed in 1927 while attempting to break the world land speed record at Pendine. As a child I must have spent hours digging in the sand, searching for the car which was buried on the beach after Parry-Thomas died.

Pembroke Dock, the junction of Meyrick Street and Bush Street. The spire of St John's Church sits behind what were then known as the 'gas showrooms'.

Occasionally, if we were lucky, we might see a grey seal sunning himself on one of the large buoys that dotted the river while herring gulls wheeled and screamed overhead. The ferry boat would pick its way past the great white Sunderland flying boats moored like lumps of chalk out in the stream and if, by chance, one was taking off we would lie, moribund, in the centre of the Haven until it had lumbered into the air.

The flying boat station closed at the end of the 1950s but for all my early childhood those huge Sunderland aircraft seemed to dominate the water off Pembroke Dock.

The base – PD as it was known throughout the service – had carried out sterling work during the war, helping to clear the western sea lanes of German U-Boats, but in the post-war world of jet aircraft and guided missiles the Sunderlands were obsolete and of little use. In 1957 the deep-throated roar of those Merlin engines were heard for the last time in the town.

A trip on the ferry was a magical experience. Years later I wrote a poem about the boats, trying to capture the excitement and the thrill of it all:-

All childhood they were there,
Convoy-steady on the Haven,
The *Lady Magdalene* and *Alumchine*,
The *Cleddau King* and *Queen*.

Sea dogs us, each Saturday
We'd make the crossing,
Leaning on the rail
Or noses pressed
To porthole windows
Where water, green and bilious,
Bubbled like a diver's nightmare
Beyond the strengthened glass.

Later, acne-blighted,
Riven by angst, this was the trip
To test out girls, to find the ones
Who'd cope with wind like demons

Ferry boats were an important part of our lives. They were, before the County Council decided to build a bridge, the only way to cross the Haven. This shows the paddler *Cleddau Queen* arriving at Hobbs Point in the summer of 1956. Notice – very few cars on board in those far-off days.

The ferry boat *Alumchine* is shown here, discharging cars and passengers. It is low tide and the only way on or off the ferry is via a very steep ramp, hazardous at the best of times, terrifying when the tide was out.

Mum and me on board the *Alumchine* on a trip across the Haven.

Pembroke Dock continued as a flying boat base for several years after the war, the giant Sunderlands lying at anchor in the river. This shows not just the flying boats but also the base itself, built in the eastern half of the old dockyard.

Through their beehived hair.
Most squealed and ran for shelter,
Consigning me – and ferry boats –
To unlamented memory.

And later still they took me,
Tremulous and daunted,
To my first job. For years
I marked class essays
As the ferry's bows
Bit deeply into Haven swells.

These days there is a bridge,
Fast and functional;
The ferries have been scrapped,
No *Mary Rose* reprieve for them.
The crossing's quicker
But romance is dead.

And children of the town
Are poorer for their passing
In this, the age of the immediate.

After a quick glass of Corona pop in the café at Neyland we'd be back on the ferry. If the weather was bad, so much the better as the boat rolled with the swells and white foam and spray patterned our coats and faces.

Once every two or three months Dad decided it was time for an extra treat. Instead of the ferry boats we took the train – a steam train, naturally – to Whitland or even Carmarthen. The trip lasted an hour or more, clouds of steam rolling down the trackside, cows and horses racing away from the thundering juggernaut. Anne and I – and for a brief period before I grew too old, too sophisticated to be seen out with my father and sisters, Judith, too – would race up and down the corridor in excitement.

We had an hour's wait at Whitland, more if our destination was Carmarthen, and that meant another glass of Corona in the buffet room, followed by a quick walk down the line to the engine shed. There we would gaze in awe at the silent, waiting engines. Then it was back to Pembroke Dock.

Occasionally, perhaps once a year, there was an extra-special treat. Then we would take the ferry boat across the Haven and catch a train from Neyland, up to the county town of Haverfordwest. From there it was another train to the port of Milford. The fishing fleet was still operating in those days, the town then being classified as the sixth-largest fishing port in the country.

Anne and me at Pembroke Dock station, ready to take one of dad's monthly trips to Whitland or Carmarthen.

The bridge outside Carmarthen, a familiar sight to us. A GWR pannier tank is about to cross the bridge over the river.

The town of Milford, where I later went to teach. In the 1950s and '60s it was still a major fishing port and a place where Anne and I went many times on trips with Dad.

One of the Milford trawlers about to enter harbour after a long haul out in the Atlantic.

We would lean on the wall or the railings above the harbour and stare in wonder at the tiny trawlers and drifters, vessels no bigger than the ferry boats that took us across the Haven, as they butted in and out of the dock. The thought of these tiny vessels enduring storms and gales out in the Atlantic filled me with romantic visions of bravery and human endurance, of the nobility and honesty of man in competition with the elements.

Years later I began my teaching career in the town and I quickly realised that deep-water fishing was one difficult and dangerous way to earn a living. Many of the children I taught came from fishing families and the poignancy of 'The Sailors Hymn' with its appeal to help 'Those in peril on the sea' put everything into perspective. Romance had no place in such an existence, but for a young boy with adventure in his soul – not to mention a soaring and undoubtedly misplaced imagination – the trawlers were the very incarnation of British sea-faring tradition.

When my sisters and I were young, they were glorious excursions, those ferry boat and train trips. They made us feel very special. Above all, they made us feel wanted and very close to that magical figure of my father. Yet when I bothered to look around, I was conscious that we were not alone. So many other fathers – always fathers, never mothers – were out with their children on those Saturday mornings. It was as if they had been working hard all week and this was their chance of a little quality time with their offspring. It was all so different from the role and behaviour of fathers these days. Hindsight and rose-tinted spectacles, maybe, but it was a wonderful world, one that seems now to have been totally unselfish.

Chapter Four
Passing Seasons

Looking back, it seems now that we had little sayings or customs for almost every time of year and occasion.

The first day of the month always saw us vying to be the quickest, the first, to take a pinch out of our friends' arms – followed by a hefty swipe across the bicep. 'A pinch and a punch for the first of the month – and no back answers,' we would wail.

November 5th? 'Remember, remember the fifth of November, gunpowder, treason and plot.' There was more but we could never remember the lines. The first frost of the year was invariably greeted by a poem – 'Watch out, watch out, Jack Frost is about, he's after your fingers and toes.'

Some of the rhymes we quoted at each other were shouted out just because we liked the sound of the words. They did not make sense but, to our ears, they sounded wonderful. Things like the ubiquitous 'How much oil would a gumboil boil if a gumboil could boil oil?' Hardly worthy of Edward Lear or Lewis Carroll, but we rolled it off our tongues like a mantra.

Girls had skipping rhymes or lines they chanted as they played hopscotch and other games but we viewed them only with disdain. For us boys, our nonsense verse was far more memorable than their rhymes or, for that matter, things like Wordsworth's 'Daffodils' or Tennyson's 'Charge of the Light Brigade' that Mrs Rees insisted we learn by heart in school. Our favourite was a version of the old music hall ditty 'In the Workhouse on Christmas Day'. Forget poignancy and sentiment, our version was far more prosaic:-

It was Christmas Day in the Workhouse,
It was snowing slowly fast
When a bare footed man with clogs on
Came slowly whizzing past.
He came round a straight bended corner
To see a dead donkey die.
He took out his gun to stab him
But the donkey cobbed in his eye.

'Cobbed' was a good Pembrokeshire dialect word meaning to spit. It was not quite respectable, one of the reasons we enjoyed chanting it. We loved the wordplay and the cadences, the nonsense of its language. It was silly and it was common, but it was unmistakeably ours!

We played conkers in the autumn – no thought of health and safety or injury then – and marbles whenever someone decided it was marbles season again. Marbles season seemed to alter every single year.

My sister Anne and me; a studio shot taken in about 1954/55.

Pembroke Street in the town on market day – always a Friday. The market, built by the Admiralty in the 1820s, is on the right of the photograph, complete with advertising signs for coming attractions at the Grand Cinema.

The one festival that never changed, of course, was Christmas. In our town Christmas began shortly after Bonfire Night. Not immediately, of course, but soon as we had time to gather the burnt out remnants of the rockets and the plastic tops of spluttering, nameless fireworks. Like witches claws we stuck them on the end of every finger.

Bonfire Night itself was just a momentary interlude, a time of building bonfires and leaping around the dancing flames like dervishes, whirling in and out of the darkness beyond the fire's glow. I remember the colours – of the fire, of the exploding fireworks – but mostly I remember the smell.

It was the smell of winter, a dark coldness mixed with the stench of smoke and what we all called gunpowder. Penny bangers were our stock in trade and it has never ceased to amaze me how, if you held one until it began to spark or fizz – not something to be encouraged or recommended – you could drop it into water and it would not go out.

Beside our back-door we had an enormous tin rainwater butt, 5 or 6 feet tall. We would light our bangers, drop them into the rain butt and call for my grandfather. He usually arrived at the door just as the fireworks exploded in columns of spray, better than a whole series of depth charges. Grandfather fell for it every time and would retire to the kitchen soaking wet, cursing our mindless stupidity.

Bonfire Night was at best a transitory time, but Christmas, oh Christmas was the joy of the year. From mid-November we hummed the seasonal weeks away, desperate for the Christmas decorations, eager to make our carol-singing-way along the darkened streets. Christmas, it seemed, would never come. Then, at last, Mrs Rees would stand before the class and intone, 'We will now make Christmas cards.' It was her one variation from the mind-numbing diet of IQ tests, maths problems and English compositions. It was, I suppose, her sop to the season – even Mrs Rees had to acknowledge the birth of Jesus Christ. Mind you, she didn't exactly do much, just shoved a pile of old Christmas cards under our noses, a few sheets of card, and let us cut, glue and paste to our hearts' content. It's the smell of that glue that remains in the memory – and the fact that you could peel it off your hands and fingers in long white strands. It was a sensory pleasure that every single one of us enjoyed.

They were hardly works of art, our cards, but they were made with love – love of the season more than anything else. We took them home and dutifully issued them to all our relatives. I even sent some of mine to my father's parents in Wickham, just outside Newcastle, where Nanny and Grampy Carradice, as I called them, were then living, Grampy working as the local police sergeant. In return I used to receive wonderful commercially produced cards, festooned with glitter and showing boys and girls preparing for Christmas, scenes worthy of any Enid Blyton story.

Breaking up for Christmas holidays was a time of great joy, a combination of relief, release and expectation. The feeling in your stomach on that final morning is almost indescribable. A hollow like a dragon's cave is the closest I can get. Bob and I would dance around school, planning all our activities and moves for the next two weeks.

The one thing we didn't plan for was Christmas Day. No planning was required. In those less commercial times Christmas Day was a day for family. The pubs were all shut, the streets dead and empty and nobody moved from the house.

It was such a culmination of weeks of worrying and planning that, inevitably, there was always a sense of anti-climax. These days children get so much for Christmas but

Grampy Phillips at the back door of
No. 41, carrying two rather large haunches
of meat. The rainwater butt where we
used to drop penny bangers to soak him is
behind him while the old corrugated iron
shed on which, as boys, we used to climb
lies further down the garden.

Christmas card, sent by my father's parents from distant Newcastle.

then money was tighter and there simply weren't the number of toys available. So whether or not you would get your cherished dreams was always as much about luck as it was about parental judgement. No wonder we believed in Santa Claus for longer than children of today.

When I was still very young my father read to me, on Christmas Eve, an abridged version of Dickens's *A Christmas Carol*. I was hooked and thereafter ploughed my way through every book the man ever wrote. I loved them all, but no character could ever quite match up to the old miser Scrooge, even if he did undergo a magical transformation three quarters of the way through and so lose most of his appeal.

The other story that enthralled me at that time of year was the Christmas story, the birth of Christ. Its simplicity and its awesome power to bring tears, of joy and sadness, to the eyes remains with me. Even now, each Christmas Eve I manage to put aside my historian's cynicism and stand in the garden, gazing up at the night sky, and know that 2,000 years ago this night the world changed.

Of course I know the date has been altered, moved to mid-winter for the sake of expediency, but the symbolism of the night is what counts. I did try to catch the feel of the moment in a short poem I was once commissioned to write for a glossy, up-market magazine. They did publish the poem, but I don't know if they understood the real meaning of the verse:-

Soft silence before midnight,
Then booming of the bells,
Bring home the Christmas message
And show that all is well.

And so it must have been that night,
The watchers waiting, ranged
In silent understanding as
The world, forever, changed.

Palestine, naturally enough, is a hot country but in my memory there was always snow at Christmas, snow and postmen slithering along the deep-rutted pavements. As Christmas Day drew nearer there were three and sometimes four deliveries in a day. On Christmas Day itself the letters still came.

The Christmas postman was always gathered into the porch for 'a little something to keep you warm'. Most houses did the same. God knows what state he was in by the end of his round.

One of the best things about Christmas was the sudden appearance in the house of what mum used to call 'Christmas provisions'. Food was never in short supply in our house – one advantage of farmhouse living – but suddenly, in the second or third week of December, we were almost overwhelmed by boxes of food and drink.

My sisters and I would rush to unpack the jars of pickled onions and red cabbage. I hated cabbage; Mum had a job and a half to make me eat even one leaf of the stuff, but red pickled cabbage? I would wolf it down.

Christmas was always a magical and inspiring time of year, a time of good cheer and overly sentimental cards.

There were boxes of Smiths Crisps, tin boxes like Jack Howard had in his shop down the road. There were apples and oranges, pears and, luxury of all luxuries, huge round pomegranates that we used to eat so carefully, extracting each seed on the end of a pin. For some reason, there were never bananas, but there were tins of ham, boxes of biscuits and even a single tin of shortbread for my Scottish father. Chestnuts to roast on the open fire and bottles of fire-hot ginger wine – it was a wonderland worthy of Dickens's Ghost of Christmas Present.

Looking back I think it was as much the season as the appearance of so much food – it certainly wouldn't have made half such an impression if it had all been delivered in, say, March or September, but food and drink were still important to all of us in those post-rationing days.

I can just about remember milk being delivered straight from the can by Kenny Scourfield who kept the farm up the road. It didn't last long and the advent of clinking milk bottles soon began to disturb all our early morning slumbers – undoubtedly more efficient and healthy, the milk now being TB tested, but nowhere near as atmospheric.

I remember the Corona pop lorry that came around the streets once a week in the late afternoons, after all the children had come home from school. For some strange reason Dad took against the sparkling fizzy drink, even though he invariably bought it for us on our trips on the train and ferry boats. 'Orange juice,' he would declare. 'Orange juice is much better for you.'

It might have been but it wasn't nearly so much fun. I used to envy Stephan and my cousin Ken, they had bottles of the stuff in their houses. It was a great day indeed if, with Dad late home from school, I could persuade my mother to buy a few bottles of orange, raspberry or, joy of joys, dandelion and burdock. 'Don't tell your father,' she would insist – although quite how we were supposed to conceal the heavy glass bottles with their swing tops, somehow managed to escape me.

Lots of food and drink was delivered by van or lorry in the early '50s, before the advent of supermarkets destroyed such initiatives. Bread and sticky buns came courtesy of Mr Rogers the baker, once or twice a week. There were even meat, vegetable and fish vans, all plying their trade in outlying places like Pennar and Llanreath. Mum didn't use them much. She had her regular order with Rees's shop in town – much posher all round, she used to say.

Papers, of course, were a different matter. They were delivered each day by poor old Mr Leonard who, with his brother, ran a newsagent's shop on Bethany Corner. He wore a long, battered raincoat, had a speech impediment and rarely spoke, but he grinned happily each time I raced towards him, unable to wait for his slow progress down the road with my weekly comic.

The *Lion*, *Tiger* and, best of all, the *Eagle* – they made the week complete. I can still feel the terrible and acute disappointment if, for some reason, they were delayed and could not be delivered. The expectation as I waited for those comics was like the expectation of Christmas, so real and alive you could almost touch it. The comics would be quickly and easily devoured and there was nothing better than sitting in the living room on a wet Saturday morning, re-reading or just flipping through my stack of back issues. Then I could read Sandy Dean's or Dan Dare's latest adventures in one complete go, rather than having to wait a week to find out what happened next.

The radio would be playing in the background as I read. No Radio One or Two in those days, my Saturday morning fare always began with Uncle Mac (Derek McCulloch to give him his full name) and *Children's Favourites*. The tunes or songs were hardly artistic masterpieces but they stay with me – 'The Laughing Policeman', 'Sparky' and 'The Runaway Train' were played, it seemed, every single week.

For years my favourite song was 'A Four Legged Friend' by the cowboy actor and singer Roy Rogers. It was a paean of praise for his horse Trigger. Later, I learned that Roy had the horse stuffed after it died and that rather destroyed the power of the song. At the time, however, it was a memorable tune.

There were other cowboy singers, people like Gene Autrey and Tex Ritter, but no-one could quite match up to Roy Rogers with his buckskin fringes and bright red suits – like no cowboy there has ever been.

Roy Rogers, the cowboy singer and actor.

There were other songs, however, and other singers. We listened to Anne Shelton warbling 'Lay Down Your Arms and Surrender to Me', Rosemary Clooney with 'This Old House' and Bing Crosby – though we would never admit to liking his too-smooth dulcet tones – and his big hit 'True Love'.

My father used to shake his head and urge my sisters and me to listen to his collection of classical records. We rarely did. Dad's one sop to light music was Vera Lynn. He never tired of praising her efforts during the war years, claiming that she had done a far better job than Gracie Fields – who had married an Italian and gone off to live on Capri – could ever have done. 'And she could sing,' Dad would say, 'which is a hell of a lot more than any of that lot can do.' He would gesture, dismissively, at the radio and bury his head in the morning paper.

Dad's prejudices were wide-ranging and all strongly held. Britain's rocket defences along the north and east coasts, ready for an attack from Soviet Russia, were pointing in the wrong direction, he claimed. 'Should be aiming across the Atlantic,' he would grunt. 'Bloody Americans!'

He hated America and all she stood for. I think it originated from his time in India and Burma where American aid and intervention were extremely limited. When Errol Flynn – actually an Australian, but Dad pretended not to notice – starred in *Burma Victory* with Stars and Stripes flying and duly won the war in the East, it roused more than a little wrathful ire in the bosoms of all British soldiers. 'We wrecked the bloody cinema,' Dad would recount with glee, 'that taught them for trying to re-write history.' Quite what a wrecked Indian cinema ever managed to do for Anglo-American or even Anglo-Indian relations, Dad never did manage to explain, but his prejudice against America was immense. Even American comics were banned in our house, *Superman*, *Batman* and the rest. And bubble gum? American trash designed to rot good British teeth! Wrigley's chewing gum; that was the stuff.

When television came along, Dad would studiously avoid all American programmes. At least he did until I came into the front room one evening – we couldn't possibly have the television set in the lounge, Mum said – and caught him surreptitiously watching the latest episode of James Garner's *Maverick*. 'Well, I suppose it is quite funny,' he managed to admit. He kept watching the series every week until, years later, the advent of home-grown programmes like *Dad's Army* and *It Aint 'alf Hot, Mum* gave him something more substantial – and something more British – to laugh about.

For a long while Uncle Freddie's farmyard was our regular playground. From early morning until the dusk began to creep in and cast long shadows across the barns and outbuildings we roamed happily through the derelict sheds. We climbed into the old haylofts and built dens out of bits of wood and string; but the greatest fun came when we tried our hands at apple fishing.

Next door to the farm lay Mr Roberts's garden. Every August his fruit trees were full of huge green apples, far too tempting for us to ignore. By weighting a line or piece of string with a rock we could create very effective fishing lines.

We would climb up the inside of the barn and push out our heads and arms through cracks in the wooden wall. Our position might be precarious, balancing high up on the rickety wall, but it gave us a beautiful vantage point, overlooking the garden. A quick cast and our makeshift lines coiled around a branch, which we would then pull

Ships and boats were an integral part of growing up. We sailed and rowed on the rivers and even when just walking on the river banks there were always vessels to see – my first ever published story was about one of these ships.

towards us. Gleefully we would strip off all the fruit before letting the branch snap back into position. They were cooking apples and they tasted bitter but they were forbidden fruit and so all the more desirable.

Dad was not happy about our illicit 'apple scrumping', but he was always willing to join us in our games, particularly when we played cricket in the back yard. He wasn't the best of batsmen, but he reduced us all to hysterics the time he took careful guard against grandfather's bouncers. 'Get down the garden to field,' he told me. 'This one's going into the river!' He promptly smashed the ball straight through the kitchen window.

Mostly we played cricket in the road outside No. 41, using one tall lamppost as the wicket and the width of the road as our pitch. For years I was a wizard at bowling slow leg-breaks, turning the ball off a sixpence and bamboozling any batsman who cared to face me. When we went to grammar school and I tried the same thing I was hit for six every time. I just couldn't understand it.

Years later I went back to that makeshift pitch and realised that the road measured exactly 19 yards in width. It meant that when I bowled my usual delivery I was a good 3-yards short – in effect delivering an old fashioned long hop. No wonder I got smashed all over the place. At least I had the satisfaction of knowing I was the best 19-yard bowler in town!

If there was a downside to what was, clearly, an idyllic childhood it came in the shape and form of the school bully.

His name was Godfrey and for years he terrorized me and, perhaps to a lesser extent, my friends as well. He was a tall beanpole of a boy with prominent teeth and I hated him and feared him in equal measure. I must have given away dozens of Dinky cars and other playthings, whatever he demanded, rather than face the fury of his fists.

One day in particular I remember. Ken, Stephan and I were playing in Uncle Freddie's farmyard when Godfrey and two of his myrmidons suddenly appeared in the entrance to the yard. I can still remember the sudden lurch in my stomach when I saw them approach.

Godfrey had some sort of gun that fired table tennis balls – not particularly dangerous but they certainly stung when they hit a bare leg or arm.

At Godfrey's direction we were herded into the back of an old van that had been parked in the lee of the barn. Every so often Godfrey's gun would appear in a gap and he would fire while we squealed and pretended to be enjoying the game. When he had used up all his ammunition we simply but stupidly threw them back to him! And so it went on until one afternoon, I reached breaking point and refused to stand out of the way as he came past. Quite why I did that, why I chose that particular moment to make a stand, I will never know but it resulted in the inevitable challenge. 'After school,' Godfrey threatened. 'You and me, we'll sort this out once and for all.' I didn't trust myself to speak but nodded and began to count off the seconds to the end of the school day.

That evening we met at the back of the school, him and his second, me and my cousin Ken. We grappled and I was amazed to find he was nowhere near as strong or as vicious as I had feared. There was no blood, no all-consuming waves of pain and no relentless battery from his fists. In fact his punching and wrestling were as ineffective as mine. After a few minutes his friend shouted a warning. 'Mrs Rees is coming!' There was no sign of her, but Godfrey and I immediately stopped struggling and made a great show of smoothing down our rumpled jumpers.

'Want to stop?' he asked. I shrugged.

'It's up to you.'

He nodded and we stood apart, panting. He stuck out his hand and I shook it. Then he went his way, I went mine and he never bothered me again.

Yours truly, a photograph taken just before I moved up to Pembroke Grammar School.

Chapter Five

Holidays

Holidays in those immediate post-war years were a rare luxury. Throughout the fifties and well into the sixties they were something that most people aspired to but rarely achieved. I suppose we were lucky and each summer we would pack ourselves into the train – Mum, Dad, Anne, Judith and me – and make an interminable journey up to Newcastle where Dad's parents were then living. I don't know what it cost; I just took it all for granted.

The trip across the broad belly of Wales and then up the spine of England took nearly twenty-four hours but it was a magical journey of steam and smoke and grime. It was a trip that was punctuated by regular changes of train and cups of tea plundered from station buffet rooms at places like Whitland, Craven Arms, Crewe and York.

I would spend the hours reading my comics – regularly replenished from the platform newsagent's whenever we changed trains – and by watching for buzzards on the tops of the telegraph poles at the side of the track. It still amazes me how the wires between those poles dipped and swung in regular motion as we thundered past.

The holidays were one long month of pleasure, of trips to Whitley Bay, Whitby or Scarborough, exciting crossings over the Tyne on the South Shields ferry or long car journeys out into the Scottish borders. It was here, on the Borders, that I first saw a curious bird with flaming coloured feathers that scuttled away into the heather as we approached. Grampy Carradice sagely informed me it was a grouse and then proceeded to tell me all about 'the glorious twelfth'.

We visited castles like Bamburgh and Alnwick or travelled by bus into Newcastle itself. The Tyne Bridge, the Swing Bridge and the shipyards which, even then, were in the last throes of prosperity offered me a new and fascinating world.

And afterwards, back home in Wickham, Grampy Carradice would encourage me in my reading, introducing me to authors like Maurice Walsh, the man who wrote the story that was later made into the John Wayne film *The Quiet Man*. Of course, it was in those wonderful summer days that I first read John Buchan's masterpiece *Huntingtower*. After reading that, for the rest of the holiday I was Dickson McCunn or Wee Jaikie, stalking the Russian agents through the fields and forests on the outskirts of the town.

Once Grampy retired from the police force, he and Nanny Carradice came to Pembroke Dock to live. Newcastle disappeared from my vision but now it was replaced with holidays in their native Scotland.

Our initial destination was Glasgow. Into the Central station we rolled, followed by a quick walk to the Broomilaw where we would board the waiting pleasure steamer, the *Queen Elizabeth 11* if I recall rightly. From there we would cruise down the Clyde, calling at exotically named ports or landing stages like Dumbarton or Dunoon, until we finally arrived in Rothesay.

A family photograph taken while on holiday in the garden of Nanny and Grampy Carradice's house just outside Newcastle.

Dad and me on the deck of a ferry boat across the Tyne at South Shields.

A trip along the River Tyne was always one of the highlights of holidays in Newcastle. This shows the famous Tyne Bridge with the Swing Bridge and the High Level railway and road bridge in the background.

After that it was three weeks of cruising along and around the Clyde, on paddle steamers like the *Jennie Deans* and *Waverley* or turbine ships like *The Duchess of Hamilton*. We would visit Cambletown and Broddick, Largs and Millport, revelling in the sea spray and the spume, the scenery and the fresh air. They were magical days and it seemed as if they would last forever. I did not know that the Clyde steamers were enjoying a last brief flowering before economics and the lure of foreign holiday destinations destroyed their world forever.

When I was nine Uncle Jim and Aunty Ave moved away from Pembroke Dock, taking their children, Ken and Chris, with them. Jim had got himself a job in the expanding steel works at Port Talbot, 100 miles to the east of Pembrokeshire. It meant financial security for him and his family and was too good an opportunity to miss.

One August morning Uncle Jim loaded his cases and his family into the familiar Vauxhall and headed off to a new house and a new life in the mysteriously named town of Pyle. It was the start of the inevitable break-up of close-knit family groups and while the initial pain of missing my cousin Ken was immense, it did at least give the family another holiday destination.

Now we could add Pyle and Kenfig Hill – I loved the names, right from the start – to the places we could go each holiday. With Jim and Ave's home as our base we took trips on the Campbell's steamers, the White Funnel Fleet as the ships were known, from Porthcawl and Penarth over the channel to places like Weston-super-Mare (Weston-super-Mud, as Dad called it), Ilfracombe and, joy of all joys, to distant Lundy Island.

On a clear day you could see Lundy from Tenby. It sat in the estuary, seemingly miles away, and from the beginning it had intrigued me. Now, with Pyle as our base, the island was suddenly far more accessible than it had ever been.

Lundy, a bleak and rugged lump of rock in the middle of the Bristol Channel, was a place of romance and adventure. In the thirteenth and fourteenth centuries it had been the haunt of the Marisco pirates – until their leader William de Marisco was captured and hung by the king.

Much to my grisly delight I read, in some travel book of the time, how the pirates' captives had been hurled from the high cliffs at the western end of the island. Despite being a good 70 or 80 miles away, if I listened carefully, on a clear, still night I was sure I could hear their screams as they plummeted down to their deaths on the rocks below.

The battleship *Montague* had been wrecked on Lundy in 1905, battered to death by the waves and wind on the rocks of Shutter Point. At low tide, from the top of the adjacent cliffs you could just pick out the last outlines of the ship's metal keel. Lundy was dark and mysterious, a place of smugglers, pirates and sudden gales – small wonder it fascinated me!

The White Funnel Fleet – by the late 1950s it had been reduced to just two vessels, the *Cardiff Queen* and the *Bristol Queen* – might not have had the appeal of the Clyde steamers, but its field of operations was certainly a lot closer. Sometimes, perhaps two or three times a year, the ships even called at Tenby to pick up passengers for an inevitable trip out to or, if the weather and tides were unfavourable, around Lundy Island. Dad, my sisters and I tried always to be there, waiting on the breakwater, if not to take the trip then certainly to see the paddle steamer.

At Wemyss Bay on the Clyde, about to embark on one of the Clyde ferries. From left to right:-
Grampy Carradice, Anne, Mum, Judith and me.

The *Waverley* was originally a Clyde paddler. She is shown here in later days, just leaving the
pier at Penarth on the Bristol Channel.

Lundy Island, dark, mysterious and foreboding. Once the haunt of pirates and smugglers, the island always fascinated me.

HMS *Montague*, aground on the rocks of Shutter Point and about to be smashed to pieces by the waves. Dockyard maties from Pembroke Dock spent months on the island, trying to free the vessel. It was no use and when the order to abandon the attempt came through they celebrated by breaking into the stores and stealing all the alcohol they could find.

The move of Uncle Jim and his family to the Port Talbot area also gave us another holiday delight – Barry Island. It wasn't long before I had fallen in love with the place, the sands (in reality, far less lordly than my own Pembrokeshire beaches), the swimming pool at Cold Nap and, in particular, the funfair.

The funfair was a glory for any young boy. There was such a thrill in the dodgems, the penny arcades and all the wild and exciting rides on offer. I can still feel the shiver of excitement as the car paused at the top of the log flume before plunging 50 feet into a world of spray and deluging water. Years later I took my wife there and tried to explain what it was about the place that was so appealing. I failed dismally and so resorted to the medium I knew best. I wrote a poem about the place:

We went to Barry Island, where the chip bags blow like rain
Along the sand-strewn gutter and the Gift Shops mark like Cain.

We went to Barry Island for a day of long-lost dreams,
For candy floss and funfairs and remembered childhood screams.

We went to Barry Island and at noon the rain came down.
It cloaked the empty beaches and the nearby dying town.

We went to Barry Island when the sea and sky were black,
When the trippers all departed and the coaches all turned back.

We went to Barry Island and we sat there in the rain,
Holding hands in the shelter and I was young again.

Perhaps it was the sentiment of the last verse, perhaps it was the word pictures, but she seemed to understand my emotions.

I suppose we were lucky, my family and I. Most people did not even contemplate summer breaks like the ones we enjoyed. For most – and, as far as the rest of the summer holiday period was concerned, for me as well – it was simply a case of picnics on the Barrack Hill or on Llanreath Beach. Maybe we would catch the bus to Freshwater East. It was our nearest sandy beach and the bus stopped at the top of a steep hill. It meant a trudge down over the dunes to reach the sand but it was worth it. The only downside lay in the fact that we had to climb back up the hill at the end of the day.

Freshwater East was a bit of a treat, a rare visit that we always enjoyed. Llanreath beach and the shingle strand along the edges of Pembroke River – a mile away, at most, from home – were our usual haunts. The water was muddy and grey and the slime oozed between our toes as we inched out into the tepid water but we didn't care.

My mother had expressly forbidden me to swim in Pembroke River. There had been a major disaster on that stretch of water between Bentlass and Lower Pennar in 1889, so long ago I couldn't even contemplate it, but the event stayed in people's memories. One grey winter day the small ferry boat that used to carry passengers from Castlemartin and Monkton across the river to the market at Pembroke Dock had gone down in a welter of crinolines and parasols. Fourteen people were drowned.

The *Cardiff Queen*, pride of the White Funnel Fleet, goes full speed astern in order to leave the tidal jetty and harbour at Tenby.

Barry Island funfair, a place of magic and mystery for any young child.

There had been other deaths in the river. Only a few years before, my friend Bob lost his aunt when she was drowned trying to save a boy who had got into difficulties in the treacherous current. Mum was terrified it would happen to me – hence the ban.

Of course, I ignored her. With my friends and, before he moved away, my cousin Ken, we swam from the walls of the old dockyard. Jacobs Pill had been a private yard that had once built the first armoured warship in the Japanese Navy. The dockyard didn't last long and by the time I was old enough to venture near the place only a few old walls and the remains of the dock gates were left, floundering and forlorn in a sea of mud, but when the tide was in they were great to dive from – as long as you took care not to smash your head into one of the lumps of concrete that still lay on the river-bed.

We also swam off the Ridge, the long finger of shale and shingle that jutted out into the river almost opposite Bob's old house. Then we dried off by running along the beach before heading for home, innocent and happy.

The Ridge was also the site of the annual Pennar Regatta. Regattas were common enough around Pembroke Dock in those years; Llanreath held one and so did Front Street in the town itself. They were little more than a series of races between sailing boats or dinghies and for those of us who watched from the shore we had little idea what was happening, but it was an event, something to break up the year. Besides, there was always a fête and gala taking place at the same time. That was a lot more fun with sideshows and races and stalls to raid. It was at the Pennar Regatta Fête that I first witnessed a slow bicycle race, contestants wiggling and jerking their wheels to keep upright and so make the finishing line last!

We also swam at Hobbs Point, the jetty where the ferries to Neyland docked – and here, I think, my mother did have a point when she threw up her hands in horror whenever I told her what I was about to do. Hobbs Point was – and is – a huge, stone jetty, originally the fitting-out berth for the old dockyard. So it was surrounded by plenty of deep water and this meant we could leap 10, 15, sometimes even 20 feet from the top and plummet into the waves. Best of all, however, was when the ferry approached.

The *Alumchine* and the *Cleddau Queen* were paddle steamers. When they approached the landing stage their paddles churned up the water in a frenzy of white foam. We would leap into the maelstrom, invariably being thrown around like toys or rag dolls in the water. The ferry men and the passengers screamed dire warnings at us, even abuse, but we ignored them. It was stupid and dangerous but, by God, was it fun!

Every October Pembroke Fair would be held in the main street of the old town. The fair was a throwback to the days of hiring fairs but by the time I arrived it was simply an excuse to enjoy the coconut shies and dodgem cars, to ride the big wheel and over-indulge on candy floss and ice cream.

The fair was set up in Main Street, the town's only real roadway, and the stalls and rides, the barkers' tents and the chip vans took over the place for a complete week. At the time I didn't notice or care but now I do wonder how the people who lived along Main Street managed to cope with the noise and inconvenience of it all.

Dad hated the fair. He knew it would mean meeting and talking to parents and pupils from school – something he really did not need on his night off. Anyway, the

The wonderful and empty sands of Freshwater East are shown in this view from Trewent Point. There is barely a soul on the beach and the dunes lie empty, apart from the odd holiday bungalow.

A family outing to the shingle beach at Llanreath – there is bound to be a kettle quietly brewing somewhere just out of shot.

The remains of the old dockyard at Jacobs Pill on Pembroke River, a place that once built ships for the Japanese Navy. The lock gates and a few pieces of broken masonry are all that remain of a once prosperous business.

An old Victorian mooring bollard on the ramp at Hobbs Point. Diving from the edge of the jetty was one of our great pleasures.

The *Alumchine* is seen here approaching Hobbs Point. The wash from her paddles created a maelstrom of foam and swirling water. Diving into this was fun but, in hindsight, decidedly dangerous.

whole procedure grated on his Scottish soul. The thought of spending money on fake rides that would last a few minutes and would then be gone forever left him cold and unmoved. He would inevitably promise all sorts of treats and prizes rather than have to take me there. 'I'll buy you a Dinky Toy aeroplane,' he would offer, 'instead of going to the fair.' 'Two,' I would counter. It was a done deal and I'd happily pocket my prizes; then I would start to work on my mother. Everyone else was going, I would tell her, all my friends – I'd be the only boy in school not to visit the fair. When my sisters came along they simply added to the pressure.

'We've got to take them, Jack,' Mum would say. 'After all, it is just once a year.' Dad would sigh with resignation, knowing he had been outmanoeuvred once again. I think, truth be known, he quite enjoyed the process.

Pembroke Fair! Like everything else it was the expectation that was best of all. We would wait all week for the Friday night when, with no school the following day, we would be allowed to stay up late. As the evening drew in and darkness began to fold itself like a blanket around the house, it was impossible to keep a grin off your face. 'Soon be time,' I would tell my sisters, 'soon be time.' Then it was coats on and we were flying through the door, out into the darkness. We would travel into Pembroke by one of the Silcox buses, hopping off at the Mill Bridge, which was as far as any traffic could go that week, and then walk up the Dark Lanes into town. We could hear the music of the waltzers and dodgems, drifting back towards us in the darkness, and everyone felt their hearts beat that little bit faster.

An old postcard view of Pembroke Fair. This photograph shows the crowds and gives a good indication of the popularity of the annual event. The whole of Main Street was – and still is – given over to the fair for a week every October.

In the early days the music was fairly traditional – the theme from *Carousel* was one I seem to remember, but as the fifties gave way to the swinging sixties the tunes took on a harder, more rocking edge. Del Shannon, Elvis Presley, Eddie Cochran – now it's impossible to separate the singers and their songs ('Runaround Sue', 'Heartbreak Hotel', 'Summertime Blues') from those haunting and enchanting nights at Pembroke Fair.

The Mill Bridge, where we decamped from the buses, stood in the shadow of Pembroke Castle, at what used to be the town's old North Gate. The Mill Pond lay on one side, Pembroke River on the other. A huge old mill – hence the name – dominated the bridge even though it had lain unused for many years. It was destroyed by fire in 1953 and although that left a much prettier view downriver, some of the atmosphere of the area disappeared at the same time. Looking back now, it is clear that Pembroke Fair appealed to all the senses, although I never realised at the time.

It began with sight, of course; the gaudy colours of the stalls and the rides, the dresses of the people, all done up in their best, as they pushed and idled through the Main Street. Then there was the sound of the blaring, jazzy music and the strident calls of the stall holders that echoed like the yodelling cries of Alpine goat herds through the night. After that came the smell of the hot dogs and the chips, the candy floss and coffee, mingled together with the pungent tang of engine oil. Always there was the feel of the cold night air on your skin. Last but certainly not least was the taste of sheer excitement. As a child you couldn't define it but that excitement was as crisp and as real as the urgent tang of Christmas morning on your tongue.

Sedate roundabout rides for younger children at the fair.

A Silcox double-decker waits at the bus stop in Albion Square, ready to take passengers into nearby Pembroke. The building behind the bus is the old Co-op offices and shop.

This photograph, taken from the walls of Pembroke Castle, shows the Mill Bridge and, on the left, the old mill itself. Long disused, this building was eventually destroyed by fire.

Two grandfathers – Phillips and Carradice – and Nanny Carradice watch the arrival of the Royal Yacht *Britannia* in 1953. My sister Anne, in her push chair, seems more interested in her ice cream.

The *Britannia* lies at anchor just off the town of Pembroke Dock. The Haven sides, in those pre-refinery days, are empty and clear.

No doubt about it, for excitement Pembroke Fair beat everything. The only event that even came close was the visit of our new queen, Elizabeth II, in 1953. She arrived in the Haven on board the Royal Yacht *Britannia* and moored just off the town. It was part of a series of visits she was making to towns around the country in order to mark her accession to the throne and for one brief week the town went 'Royalty crazy'.

We were given a day off school, there were more parties and bun fights and the Sunderlands from the RAF base made a spectacular fly-past. It was something of a swan song as soon the flying boats would be gone forever from Pembroke Dock. We stood and watched in awe. Then the queen re-boarded the *Britannia* – the first royal yacht, incidentally, not to have been built in Pembroke Dockyard – and sailed away down the Haven. For all of us in the town it was back to normal.

Part Two

Chapter Six

Secondary School

I don't suppose it's any different now, but childhood, as I remember it, was always filled with seminal moments, points that marked the end of one stage of life, the beginning of another. Moving from primary to secondary school – whether it was to grammar or secondary modern – was, perhaps, the most daunting problem many of us ever encountered. It meant leaving the security of small, familiar places and well-known people for the immensity of the unknown – even the dreaded Mrs Rees seemed, for a while, considerably less daunting.

It may not have been the right biological moment – that was still a year or so away – but in many ways moving up to secondary education actually was the end of childhood, at least the end of childhood as I knew it, and the beginning of adolescence.

It was the most significant moment of our lives although none of us knew or even suspected it at the time. These days, with comprehensive schools, the change is neither so sudden nor so dramatic. Many children remain with their childhood friends all their school days. Not so at the end of the 1950s.

I was lucky. My main friends – Bob and Kenny in particular – came with me to Pembroke Grammar, but others, on the periphery of our circle, went off to the Coronation Secondary Modern and no matter how hard we tried to keep the contacts, from that moment in time our lives went in different directions.

Pembroke Grammar lay half-way between Pembroke and Pembroke Dock, high on a ridge overlooking Pembroke River. It was newly built when I first went there, perhaps two or three years old, but, being on the side of the hill, there was already a degree of slippage. The 'powers that be' had inserted small pieces of glass into some of the walls, to monitor any movement in the building. 'I reckon that's all that's keeping the building up,' laughed Bob, prodding at one of the glass strips with his index finger. 'We'll turn up one morning and find the bloody place down in the river.'

A new school meant new experiences, new lessons and a wide range of subjects that would have left Mrs Rees gasping at their immensity.

The first morning was one of initiation – initiation into the ways of secondary education and, at break time, into the somewhat cruel rituals of adolescence. 'What does a ship do when she enters harbour?' a worldly-wise second year threw at me as we stood in the playground glancing nervously around. I shrugged. 'She ties up,' he shouted, gleefully, and flicked my tie. My eyes and hands followed the amber and black strip of cloth into the air. 'And anchors down!' the boy yelled. He stamped, hard, on my toe. I limped around for the rest of the day – but knowing that no-one could pull that particular trick on me again.

Ducking new pupils – filling washbasins with water and then shoving in the newcomers' heads – was a tradition of the school, one we endured in our first year, and

An aerial view of Pembroke Grammar School, perched on the side of the ridge between Pembroke and Pembroke Dock.

then perpetuated as we grew older. One or two of our class even had their heads forced down the toilet pan before a quick flush of the chain gave them release. Thankfully, I managed to escape such an indignity.

Pembroke Grammar School opened up a whole new world of teachers and teaching. The English, maths and IQ tests we had previously endured in primary school were augmented or, usually, supplanted by a wide range of new subject areas. Even the process of 'being educated' was different.

Previously we had been stuck in just one room with Mrs Rees holding sway over everything we thought or did. Now we roamed the school, moving from one room or subject area to another as the timetable demanded. Our form room was a refuge where we could easily and happily leave books and PE kit, with never any concern that they might be stolen or vandalized.

English literature, history and geography had an immediate appeal for me, an appeal that has never faded, but the various science labs on the ground floor of the main building put me off, right from the start. I hated the smell of those dark, eerie places with their long brown benches, rows of test tubes and Bunsen burners. One look and I quickly decided that science was not for me.

Languages like French, Latin and Welsh were just about bearable – although I quickly discovered that I had absolutely no aptitude for any of them. I was always up against the odds in art as the art teacher and my father – who did a similar job in the Coronation – were friends and colleagues. Dad's distant influence wove an invisible and unplanned spell across my artistic endeavours.

The school badge, showing Pembroke Castle with the two flags blowing in opposite directions, and the school's Latin motto – roughly translated it means 'Their glory will be seen forever.'

'But you've got to be able to draw,' Mr Cooper would complain as he stared in disbelief at my weekly effort. 'Your father is an artist – he must have passed on some of that talent to you.' I did think of telling him that my grandfather was also a farmer, but that didn't mean I would happily push my arm up the backside of a cow or sheep. Wisely, I kept my council to myself.

The teachers, we quickly discovered, were a fascinating lot. Our headmaster, T. C. Roberts, was a new incumbent – just like us, really. He had recently taken over from Roland Mathias, a Welsh poet of great skill and fame who had guided the school through the war years.

Along with Raymond Garlick, another well-known poet and English teacher at the school, Mathias had founded *The Anglo-Welsh Review*, one of the most influential and best-loved literary magazines in the country. Years later, when one of my early poems was printed in the magazine it was one of the proudest moments of my life.

T. C. Roberts was a mathematician and, for almost the whole tenure of my stay at the school, remained a distant and remote figure. We saw him at morning assembly when he would parade down the aisle, black gown flying and, for once, his mouth unadorned by the habitual cigarette stub. We would hear his nasal whine over the intercom, usually demanding that some miscreant should immediately report to his study, and sometimes see him sweeping down the corridor outside our classrooms.

We called him the 'Phant', short for the 'Phantom Pig', a sobriquet that he earned by his hunched, corpulent figure – and, it was said, by his innate ability to appear behind you whenever mischief was afoot; phantom, indeed.

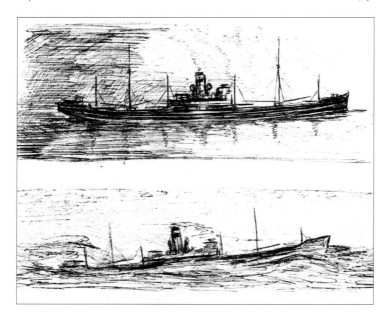

My father's skill as an artist meant that the school had great expectations of me. I was a sore disappointment.

All of the teachers wore gowns and, when the occasion demanded it – Prize Day, School Eisteddfod and the like – mortar boards as well. Without fail, they all had a wonderful range of one-liners, comments that were guaranteed to freeze you in your tracks.

I remember, when I was in the third or fourth year, some friends and I set about pulling down the cricket nets and using them, like gladiators in the arena, to enmesh and then bounce younger pupils up and down – great fun but decidedly dangerous. As one of our victims shot 15 feet into the air, the metalwork teacher, who also happened to run the cricket team, suddenly appeared behind us.

'Right, Spartacus,' he hissed at me, thumb pointing downwards in a more than passable imitation of a Roman Emperor. 'The games are over.'

We were dispatched to his metalwork room to await his pleasure. And wait we did, for nearly forty minutes, suspense and fear building and contrasting with the cleverness of his comment. When he did finally appear, six swipes across the backside with a metal ruler were more than enough to dispel any pleasure I might have got from his way with words.

The comment I remember best, perhaps because it was both clever and true, came from my Welsh master, a generous and kind-hearted man who I must have driven to distraction by my lack of skill and interest in his subject. We didn't know it then but Islwyn Griffiths was a war hero, a bomber pilot who kept his exploits and his past life to himself. To us he was just a quiet, gentle man who clearly loved his subject and ran the school branch of the Urdd youth association.

'Carradice,' he said one day as I wandered into his classroom, 'you like history, ships and that sort of thing, don't you?'

'Yes, sir,' I nodded, warily, expecting a trap of some type.

'Good,' he said. 'So tell me, what's the speed of a convoy?'

I thought about it carefully. 'I don't know, sir. Five or six knots?' Islwyn shook his head. 'No, boy, the speed of a convoy is the speed of the slowest ship – and you're it!' I

Pembroke Dock in the 1960s. Monti's Café is on the right, the entrance marked by the 'Teas and Ices' sign.

loved the comment, but I don't think it made any difference to my performance in the Welsh lessons.

A new school, of course, meant new friends. Right from the start most of my friendships were formed and centred on sport.

In primary school I had discovered that I had no talent whatsoever as far as soccer was concerned. My feet were always too far away from my brain to work properly. Cricket was all right. I could play a straight bat to most balls on a line and length and by keeping wicket I could dive about all over the place and at least look as if I knew what I was doing.

But at Pembroke Grammar we played rugby and by the time I was thirteen years old the game had become my whole reason for existence. Dennis Lloyd, our PE teacher, quickly decided that I was to play hooker. In those days hookers struck for the ball in the scrums and I was quick with my reflexes, regularly taking five or six balls against the head each game. Mind you, my hooking wasn't always strictly legal.

'You drop your left knee when you're striking,' one of our teachers, 'Thumper' Powell, told me as we made our way up to the top field for a game. 'You ought to be penalised every time you go into a scrum.' He happened to play hooker for Pembroke and often refereed our Saturday morning match before going off to play his own game in the afternoon. 'See that bandage,' he said, pointing to a white crepe bandage I had wound around my left knee. 'I guarantee it'll be black with mud by half time.' I grinned at him, cocky and full of myself. 'Then penalize me,' I said. 'Until then I'll play the ref.' That day I took twelve against the head. He never penalised me once but, true enough, my left knee was black with mud after just thirty minutes.

The Creators, *c.* 1968. From left to right:- Mike Sallis, Mark Clarke, my mate Bob Howells and Peter Mitchell. In the late '60s, the Creators were the leading rock band in the town and area.

It was through rugby that I became friendly with Bruce Penfold, Dave Eastick and Howard Robinson. They were Pembroke boys but, along with Bob and Kenny, sport brought us together in friendships that would last for the rest of our adolescence. There were others, of course, boys who had no interest in any form of sport but there was no doubt that those of us who represented the school in the Under-13s, the Juniors and, finally, the First XV saw ourselves as an elite; and, boy, did we play on it!

Of course, we played other sports as well, at varying degrees and levels of ability. Bob went on to become one of the best athletes our school ever produced, excelling at the javelin and high jump. Dave Eastick was a fast bowler of consummate skill and grace, someone who represented Wales at cricket and only his tragically early death prevented him from achieving even greater honours.

I was never a great cricketer but I did enjoy the game. Interestingly, the only real injuries I ever received on the sports field came, not as you might expect from rugby, but on the cricket pitch.

We were playing in the annual Pembroke-Pembroke Dock match, a fiercely contested rivalry that neither side wanted to lose. Bruce, Dave and Howard were playing for Pembroke, the rest of us for the 'Dock'. I was fielding at silly mid-on – and if ever there is an appropriate name for a fielding position that is it – when one of their players, a boy named Guy Pearce, smashed the ball straight at me. It shot through my grasping hands before I had time to move and hammered into my ribs. All the breath was knocked from my body, one rib was broken and the imprint of the ball's seam was there for weeks afterwards. 'You bloody clown,' hissed Bob as he stood over my prostrate body, shaking his head in disbelief. 'You dropped him!'

The other injury came in the same match the following year. I was keeping wicket, close up to the stumps. Howard Robinson, the batsman, swung at the ball and missed. He didn't miss me. The bat exploded against my head and I was carried, unconscious, from the field of play.

Bob had been given a guitar for passing his 11-plus exam – I got a bike, an old fashioned 'sit up and beg' thing that I hated from the start. I would have liked a drop handlebars machine, something speedy and sporty, but it was not to be. Before long my bike was rusting away in the old dairy at the back of my house, forgotten and unlamented. Bob's guitar, however, was something of a watershed for him.

He had real ability and within a few months was both proficient and confident. He was happy to perform – to start with just singing into his tape recorder. We used to make up radio programmes, bad versions of the *Goon Show*, or warble songs like 'Don't Jump off the Roof, Dad' into the microphone. Bob even tried to teach me how to play, but my repertoire was always severely limited – what do you expect with a range of just three chords?

By the time he was fifteen Bob was playing in one of the local rock bands that our town had spawned. He could sing, too, and that made him ideal material for the music scene that erupted in every town in Britain following the phenomenal success of the Beatles and the Rolling Stones.

Music was hugely important in those early 1960s. It began with people like Elvis and Jerry Lee Lewis – never Cliff Richard, he was just for the girls – and then, after 1964, we were swept up in the incredible circus that was Beatle mania. We all played

Typical teenage self-indulgence – me taking a picture of me in my bedroom mirror.

their albums on our Danset record players, pounding out the rhythms that drove our parents insane. Very few of us, apart from Bob and, later, Howard, were able to be part of that scene but we all dreamed that one day some miracle would occur and we would be transformed into pop stars. Of course, it was never going to happen but the dream was, perhaps, even more potent than the reality.

The 1960s really were a time of 'youth revolution'. Youth culture suddenly began to matter, to the press, to the businessmen who controlled it all – and to us. We would wait, religiously, for Saturday nights when we could watch *Thank Your Lucky Stars* and *Juke Box Jury* on television. Sunday afternoons were reserved, exclusively, for Alan Freeman and *Pick of the Pops*.

Before long our clothes and hairstyles were shocking and enraging the older generation, pushing us into positions or stances that were at different ends of the spectrum from our parents and teachers. I was no different from anyone else and soon

A wedding party in the garden of No. 41 – the height of the house can be clearly seen, and the extension onto which I used to climb.

I was wearing my hair long, half-way down my back – much to the disgust of my father.

'Why do you do it?' he asked.

'I want to be different,' I replied.

Dad shook his head in disbelief and pointed at me, dangerously. 'No, you don't. You want to be like everyone else. If you want to be different, have a short back and sides. Then you'd be really different. Get it cut.'

He was right, of course. I did get my hair cut – a quarter of an inch off the bottom to sort out the split ends.

For a long time, at least until the late '60s, skin-tight trousers were an essential fashion accessory. I used to get mine taken in by a seamstress in the 'Dock', wearing them so tight I could barely bend my legs to get up the stairs. Mum and Dad refused to allow me to wear them to school, but I would simply put them under my regulation school trousers and change at the bus stop.

There were times during my adolescence that my father could be a real nuisance. Being, by that stage, deputy head at the Coronation Secondary Modern he had to take assembly on a regular basis. I always knew when it had been his turn because, for days afterwards, the Coronation kids would all stop and stare at me in the street.

'What the hell are you looking at?' I would demand. Then it would come out. He had stood up in assembly and ranted on about my winkle-picker shoes, my hair style or my drain-pipe trousers, using them as examples of teenage daftness – great fun for the pupils, damned infuriating for me.

'Stop it, Dad, please?' I would urge.

'Get yourself a decent pair of shoes,' he would counter, 'then we'll see. Those things won't last five minutes.' He would point at my razor thin, Cuban-heeled footwear, shaking his head in despair. He was usually right. The soles would invariably split away from the heels after a week or so but there was no way I would tell him. I used to tape them back together with Elastoplasts. It was damned uncomfortable and I would have to slide along like a novice ice skater rather than pick up my feet like any normal human being. Dad smiled and said nothing although he did, once, ask if I was constipated or unwell. 'I'm fine, thanks,' I said. He nodded, knowingly. 'Good. It's my assembly next week – thought you might like to know.'

Chapter Seven
A Social Life

Pembroke and Pembroke Dock were small communities. It meant that we all knew each other and were able to enjoy the triumphs – and, to be honest, the disasters – of everyone and anyone. It wasn't just our own towns, either.

As teenagers we knew most of the boys from Tenby, Milford or Haverfordwest. We played rugby and cricket against them and we met them in the weekly dances at Haggar's or the De Valance. We were, quite simply, friends.

We were lucky and had lots of different places to meet up and enjoy time together. In particular there were Brown's and Monti's, two cafés that quickly became our habitual homes away from home. The 1960s was the age of coffee bars and cafés, places where we would sit for hours over a coke or a frothy coffee, putting the world to rights.

Brown's was situated in the middle of Pembroke Main Street, a long, thin restaurant lined with mirrors that showed every side of your hair, head and body every time you went in. I must have spent hours studying my reflection – surreptitiously, of course – making sure that every slicked-back hair was in place

The mirrors had another advantage. Sitting in the back section of the café you could see everyone who came in, long before they saw you. So, a girl you really did not want to meet? Hide until she'd looked around and then left in high dudgeon – politically and socially very incorrect but, some would say, a natural part of adolescence and growing up; and, of course, there was always the distinct possibility that she was doing exactly the same to you.

Brown's was a restaurant as well as a café and they produced a wonderful line in spit-roasted chickens. You could see and smell them every time you went in, the glorious aroma making your mouth water like a running tap, but it wasn't 'cool' to be found eating in a café – chips out of a bag in the street, that was fine but never seated behind a table in places like Brown's. We drooled and fretted and contented ourselves with ice-cold bottles of coca-cola. It was scant consolation.

Monti's Café was a local institution in Pembroke Dock. It was located in Dimond Street – I still don't know why there is no 'a' in Dimond – and had been owned and run by a family of Italian origin since long before the Second World War.

The Montis were just one of many Italian families who came to Wales in the 1920s. They came, in the main, from the Bardi area of northern Italy, and opened cafés and ice cream parlours in places like Treorchy and Treherbert, Ebbw Vale and Penarth, providing warmth and a little sustenance for men and women in a time of great economic hardship. In the years leading up to the war there was barely a community in Wales that did not have its own Italian café.

During the war, once Mussolini had thrown in his lot with Hitler, many of the Italian café owners were interned on the Isle of Man. That's what happened to Mr Monti.

In the days before we could drive, getting around was either by bus or train. This shows the station at Pembroke Dock – it must have been a busy day, two trains in!

Part of the interior of Brown's Café in Pembroke, complete with the essential coffee-making machine.

Within weeks of Mussolini declaring war he was whipped away, leaving his wife to continue with the business until peace came again and he was able to return once more to Pembroke Dock.

By the time I started to frequent Monti's the old man was long dead, but the business was carried on by his wife and daughters. It was a wonderful place of shining tables, a loud and colourful juke box and a stainless steel coffee machine that hissed and steamed all day long. The café was set on two levels, the upper one with a wide plate-glass window, through which we could watch the world go by, and there we were allowed to while away the hours, talking and gossiping – as long as we fished into our pockets and splashed out on the occasional coke or coffee.

It's hard to define, exactly, what Monti's meant to us in those days. It was our meeting place on Saturdays – when there was no rugby to play – and in the school holidays when the long days stretched out ahead of us like the innocent and eager moments of early childhood. I did try to capture the feelings in a poem I wrote many years later, after the café had been pulled down to make way for new developments – and of the looming threat which, quite probably, only really existed in hindsight:

> There was a time we sat
> in Monti's Café,
> each cradled cup of coffee,
> a frothing Mount Vesuvius,
> precious as frankincense or myrrh.
> And as the juke box screamed
> "Three Steps to Heaven"
> or "Summertime Blues"
> in perfect time we'd nod
> our combed and brillcreamed quaffs.
>
> Behind us, silver and mysterious
> as any spaceship from Cape Kennedy,
> the coffee maker hissed,
> its proud Medusa wail
> filling the room with sound and steam,
> a terminus of wild excitement.
>
> All morning we'd talk on,
> hoarding cokes and coffee,
> knowing that the town was ours;
> such hedonism was our right,
> the world of work, of adult cares,
> a million miles away.
> We thought that it would last forever.
>
> There should have been a slave
> beside us as we sat,

Monti's Café in Pembroke Dock began life as a sweet shop, tobacconist and ice cream parlour. This early 1920s shot shows Mrs Monti outside the shop.

Monti's in the 1960s was like the centre of the universe. It was where we met to discuss plans and just idle away the day.

whispering that this was transient.
And like all glory
it would quickly pass.

We didn't know until
we woke one morning
to find the world had changed.
College, work, the lure
of long relationships
destroyed those dandelion days
as surely as the atom bomb
we feared one day would drop.

And nothing, nothing,
was ever quite the same again.

Brown's and Monti's were for daytime use, for an early evening drop-in, perhaps, before a trip to the pictures at Haggar's or the Grand. Adolescence was when I finally found out what the wide, double seats in the back few rows of the cinema were really all about. I must have paid for entry to dozens of films and never actually got to see even one of them – at least, not all the way through.

There was something warm and comforting about the back row, shrouded in darkness, reeking with the illicit scents of discovery. Yet again, the figure of my father rears up when I think of nights in those darkened halls. Once I made the mistake of asking him to run me into Pembroke. I was late and the girl I was due to meet – one of Dad's pupils at the Coronation – had made it quite clear, she would wait only five minutes.

'Drop me at the Mill Bridge,' I told him, not wanting him to know all my business. 'I can run from there.'

Dad did as he was asked and, taking to my heels, I managed to arrive at the front of Haggar's just in time. We were about to go in when a car horn sounded. I spun around and there was my father, leaning out of the passenger window, pointing his finger at me and wagging it meaningfully.

'Don't be late,' he called. 'Remember your mother wants to bathe you.'

The girl dissolved into laughter as, red with anger and embarrassment, I shouted abuse after the disappearing car. The date was not a success.

In hindsight we were so lucky. We didn't hang around on street corners as there were always places to go – Brown's, Monti's or the Grand. In particular, there was the Double Two.

The Double Two was a café-come-dance hall run by Mr Williams and his wife. Open seven nights a week, it stood on London Road, on the outskirts of the town and was, really, little more than a corrugated iron shack, but it was warm, filled with music from the juke box and Mr Williams tolerated no trouble.

I was no dancer, subscribing to Bob Dylan's adage that only a man who is certifiably insane or drunk out of his brain will go willingly onto the dance floor, but the Double

Haggar's Cinema in Pembroke, its popularity clearly shown by the long queue to get in – sometimes it stretched away down the hill to the Mill Bridge. The film on offer seems to be the eminently forgettable *Good Time Girl* – not that the punters had any complaints.

Two was the place to meet girls and that did, unfortunately, mean having to venture out onto the heaving wooden floor every now and then. Thank God it usually was heaving, literally – it meant that no-one could see the intricate series of tortured body jerks that, in my case, passed for dance moves. The only dance I could ever do was the Twist and even then I looked like a man with a hole in his shoe trying to grind out a cigarette stub!

The jukebox was available any time but every Wednesday night Mr Williams gave 'free plays' – which was fine, as long as you survived the scrum to get to the machine first. On Saturday nights there was a live band, usually the Valiants, a local band that would play the latest hits by people like Cliff and the Shadows. Later on, when my mate Bob joined the Creators, they played there, too.

For several years before we outgrew its alcohol-free environment – Mr Williams would allow no drink, either in his club or on the breath of his customers – the Double Two was our habitual Saturday night home. People came from all over the county to enjoy the ambience of the 'Twos', as it was known. The place really was a unique piece of social engineering.

Of course, it wasn't all perfect. There were occasional fights, usually between the German soldiers who came each year to train at nearby Castlemartin Artillery Range and those locals who firmly believed that the young German conscripts with their impeccable manners and elegant clothes were trying to steal away their girlfriends. They were probably right.

The fights invariably took place in the car park outside the Twos and usually finished after the odd blow or two. We would crowd around to watch, but that was the limit of our adolescent involvement.

The Valiants play at the Double Two, well-known local guitarist Ray Doney in the centre of the group. The café/dance hall was little more than a corrugated iron shack but it provided welcome entertainment for the youth of Pembroke and Pembroke Dock.

Sadly, one night in the early '70s, after closing, the Double Two caught fire and was burned to the ground. It left young people in the 'Dock' considerably poorer – and an older generation of past users filled with more than a little sentimental regret.

As we became more confident in our social skills my friends and I did manage to venture further afield. Haggar's Ballroom above the cinema in Pembroke held a regular Saturday night dance. It was interesting, sitting in the cinema and listening to the pounding of feet on the floor above your head – one day, I used to say, the whole lot will come through. The image of falling dancers dropping onto amazed movie goers is one that still amuses me.

As we grew older we developed a regular routine – into the King's Arms or the Lion for as many beers as we could stomach (or pay for, come to that) and then, at closing time, we would nip across the road into Haggar's for the last hour. Underage drinking is not a new phenomenon; we did it back in the 1960s. I think the difference lay in the fact that we didn't go out to get drunk. It may well have happened, but it was not the primary purpose of the exercise.

If the band playing over at Haggar's was famous we would invariably get there earlier. It was at Haggar's, for example, that I first heard the Moody Blues and, before they were really well known, the Mindbenders. They were definitely worth missing our evening drinking in Pembroke's pubs.

When we went to Tenby it was the De Valance Pavilion that was our destination. We rarely ventured as far as Haverfordwest but I do remember, once, going to a dance in Milford. Mike Berry and the Innocents were playing and when we were warned

A sad end – the Double Two after it had been destroyed by fire.

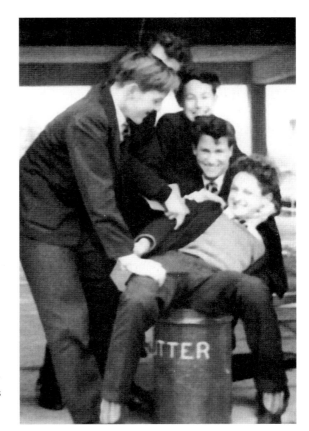

'Fun' in the covered playground at school. As someone once said, a future V-bomber pilot and soon-to-be managers and executives put future author in the bin! Left to right: Kenny Deveson, David Hughes, Bob Howells and me. Hidden behind Kenny is Howard Robinson.

off 'their territory' by a group of Milford teddy boys – who outnumbered us three to one – we decided the band wasn't good enough to risk serious injury and beat a hasty retreat back across the river.

All that, of course, came later in adolescence. When I was still in my first year at Grammar School my father founded what was euphemistically called the Railway Club. It was, really, a modelling club for boys of both the Grammar and Coronation schools.

We would meet each Thursday evening in his Art Room at the Coronation, completing intricate and detailed models of trains and aircraft. We even went on a trip to London – my first visit to the metropolis although Dad had little in mind apart from visits to places like Paddington, Euston and St Pancreas.

The Air Cadets was another outlet for our energies. Never having been a great one for things like the Cubs or Scouts I came late to the Air Cadets, following on the heels of Kenny and Bob. By then they had both achieved 'status' within the organisation, Kenny rising to the dizzy heights of Flight Sergeant and Bob to Corporal. I never made it beyond first base, but it was still a great experience. We went on weekend camps to places like St Athan and a two-week summer camp at RAF Valley on Anglesey. That was where I flew for the first time, in an old Avro Anson, and was duly sick into the regulation issue paper bag. It was at Valley that I also fired a .303 rifle for the first time.

'Watch the kick,' our instructor told us. 'These rifles have a belt like a mule, so hold them tightly and squeeze – squeeze – the trigger.'

That's exactly what I did, but unfortunately I also had my thumb raised at the same time. The recoil smashed my thumb backwards into my nose – blood everywhere, much to the amusement of the platoon and our officers.

Thinking back, it is clear that we had a whole range of organised activities available to us. If you wanted to get involved there were youth clubs in both Pembroke and Pembroke Dock but quite a lot of our evening and weekend life centred around the school – in much the same way as, earlier, they had been based around the chapel.

We attended weekly meetings of the Urdd, the Welsh youth organization, holding debates about the position and role of Wales in modern society and watching films about other young people in other parts of the world.

We also became members of the school Young Farmers' Society, the 'Green Wellie Brigade' as someone once called us.

I don't know about green wellies but I do remember being dragooned into the Young Farmers' Club folk dancing team – me and half a dozen other boys from the First XV.

'But I can't dance,' Bruce Penfold wailed.

'You'll learn,' retorted Mrs Tapley, the girls' PE teacher who was running the squad. 'Even an idiot can do this.'

I kept quiet about my own lack of ability on a dance floor and submitted meekly to her demands. The dancing was formulaic, a bit like those routines you see in film adaptations of *Pride and Prejudice* or other Jane Austen classics.

'It's like painting by numbers,' Bruce said, frowning, counting the steps and trying hard to keep his place. I nodded my agreement. 'Or working to a blueprint,' I said. 'Follow the plans and you'll be OK.'

The Railway Club outing to London, 1960, in what was, really, the last days of steam.

Pembroke Dock Air Cadets at Valley in Anglesey. I stand second from the right in the back row, Bob and Kenny are second and third from the left (seated).

It wasn't the most inspiring of exercises. I hated every minute of it but, surprise surprise, we won the competition at the annual Young Farmers Meeting in Haverfordwest – perhaps because we were following the formula so closely. Mrs Tapley tried to cajole us again for the next year, but Bruce and I had had enough and politely, but firmly, declined the offer.

For several years, from about the age of thirteen onwards, camping and even hiking became an essential part of our lives. Each summer we would take an old army bell tent, a huge and unwieldy affair that one of us had managed to acquire, out to Freshwater East and pitch it high on the dunes above the beach. There we would lounge and lord the summer away.

The first night at camp was always the best. We'd pitch the tent and then, as dusk descended across the dunes, we'd race down the beach for the first swim of the holiday.

Then we'd amble back to our campsite and dig a huge fire pit. As the flames jumped and danced around in the darkness we'd throw potatoes into the embers and lie back on the grass and watch the shooting stars as they flashed and died in the western heavens. As the poet once said, 'If there be a heaven on earth it is this, it is, this it is this.'

In those days the dunes at Freshwater East were wild and unkempt, just the occasional wooden and corrugated iron bungalow and the odd pathway down to the beach to break the rolling banks of marram grass and soft white sand. For five weeks

The dunes and beach at Freshwater East, the scene of many summer camps during the early and mid-1960s – perhaps the bell tent at the right of the picture was actually that of my friends and I.

we swam and surfed, canoed and played cricket on the beach. All the while we slowly turned a golden brown under a sun that was always hot.

We were no great shakes at cooking and, looking back, I think we survived the summer on a diet of fried eggs and beans. One set of parents would re-supply us each week, bringing out sausage rolls and cakes which we would demolish in a day before returning to our staple diet of eggs and beans.

The only trouble with Freshwater East came in the shape of snakes – adders, the only poisonous snakes in Britain. One morning we rose early in order to catch the tide. There was a strong wind blowing and the surf was high, possibly one of the best chances that summer to use our surfboards.

Down to the beach we went, walking along a narrow path between high bushes of gorse. At the bottom of the path, sunning itself in the early morning calm, there it was – the biggest adder we had ever seen. We had no idea that the snake was a lot more frightened of us than we were of him and in an instinctive movement one of the boys lashed out with his surf board. The snake was thrown up into the air and came down, smack on the top of my head.

It fell to the ground, seemed to shake itself and scurried away into the bushes. Me? I wasn't hurt, but I was traumatised – I didn't stop shaking for a week. Ever since that moment I have been terrified of snakes. It seems more than reasonable to me.

A local entrepreneur opened a night club at Freshwater East a few years after we started camping there. It was a great place to meet girls, holiday makers from places like London and Cardiff. They were usually staying in one of the bungalows that were dotted around the dunes and their parents willingly and generously supplied us with chip suppers whenever we brought their daughters back home.

Usually these friendships died the moment the girls went back home but, once, Bob and I promised to keep in touch with two girls from Cardiff. We wrote once or twice and glibly commented that we would call on them next time we were in the city – and that was exactly what we did, calling unannounced, with never a thought of what might happen if we were turned away. Amazingly, the parents of my girl let us stay, sleeping on their front room floor. The father even transported us around. Their generosity knew no bounds.

I enjoyed camping, lying out on the dunes in the evening sun, much more than sampling the delights of the club. I went along, with everyone else, quaffing the weak beer and trying hard to look as if I was enjoying it. When, however, some of my friends began taking their suits with them on our camping trips I decided it was not for me – and another stage of life came to an end.

Chapter Eight
Rugby

For some reason Pembroke Grammar School chose not to have a first year band. You went straight into the Second Form and in due course moved up to the Third, Fourth, Upper Fourth and so on. It was more than a little pretentious and, I suppose, was an attempt to ape the public school system, but it had been in existence for many years before I arrived and somebody clearly thought that it worked.

It was the same with the House system. You were assigned to one of four Houses on your arrival at the school and your subsequent life – at least, your school social life – was arranged around this framework. I was placed in Glyndwr House and just as the chapel had dominated things in early childhood, now school managed to do the same.

After-school activities occupied much of every week. Like so many of my friends, I played House rugby, House cricket, House seven-a-side and so on. I acted in House Drama Competitions and competed in the school eisteddfod – all for the honour of the House. I wrote poems and stories, gave recitations and, God forbid, even sang in the various choirs.

It was all great fun, hugely enjoyable, but by the time I reached the Upper Fourth I had realised that my talents and abilities were strictly limited. In fact the only thing I seemed to excel at was rugby.

I began to think that I might have a modicum of skill in the game when, in my third year at the school, I was suddenly elevated into the heights of the Junior XV, playing with and against boys a good twelve or eighteen months older than me. When my true Junior year arrived I found myself selected for the County XV, along with Bruce Penfold and Kenny Deveson.

Playing for Pembrokeshire Schoolboys was my first representative outing and I loved every minute of the experience. We traveled all over Wales, playing other county and regional sides, but our greatest moment came at home, on Milford's Observatory Ground in Hakin.

We were playing against Llanelli Schools and opposite me in the front row was no less a person than 'Bull' Butler who went on to gain several caps as a prop forward for Wales. Llanelli had not lost for several seasons and had not had a try scored against them for months, but ten minutes into the game we were given a lineout on their goal line. Phil James – known to all of us by the unflattering name of Fatso – crashed over to put us into the lead.

Sadly, it couldn't last. They had a mercurial little outside half who could turn on a sixpence and stop dead in his tracks, even when he was running at full speed.

'Get him into a maul,' our captain gasped, 'and beat the crap out of him!' We tried but, unfortunately, we couldn't catch him. That was my first encounter with Phil Bennett, Welsh and British Lions captain. It certainly showed us the gap between

A newspaper cutting showing Phil James scoring a try against Llanelli Schoolboys. I am in the centre of the photograph, posing as usual – well, if you can't score yourself, make sure you're around when the photographer takes the snap!

merely good and great. And, of course, guided by Bennett, Llanelli went on to win in the final quarter.

In due course I moved up into the school (and County) First XV, one of my earliest games being – yet again – against Llanelli. This time they had future Welsh international and, if I remember rightly, future American football star Terry Price in their ranks. It was men against boys and they duly put us to the sword.

We didn't mind the beating but when the Phant stood up in assembly the following Monday morning and berated us for letting down the school, like most of the team I was mortified. For a while I wondered which planet he came from and seriously considered giving up playing for the school. Of course I didn't – for which I am eternally grateful.

Perhaps the most memorable match in my first year for the senior side was against Gwendraeth. My friend Roger McCallum – 'Mush' as he was known to all and sundry without any of us seeming to know why – was playing flanker. Their outside half ran us ragged and at half-time Mush collapsed onto the turf, gasping for breath.

'You're not fit, Mac,' said Idris Cleaver, our woodwork teacher and County selector who happened to be on the line watching. 'You need to spend a bit less time in the back row of the Grand and a bit more in the gym.'

'Who is that bloody outside half?' Mush panted. 'I can't lay a finger on him.'

'You're not ever likely to,' said Idris. 'That's Barry John.' If he'd had the energy Mush would have groaned out loud. As he later said, that was the moment he knew Barry John had come of age.

My first year in the school First XV. I am sitting on the ground, second from the left, next to Kenny Deveson. Bruce Penfold sits far right. Roger McCallum stands fourth from the right in the back row. The staff are Dennis Lloyd and, in gown, the Phant – T. C. Roberts.

By the time I was seventeen I was playing two games every Saturday, turning out in the morning for the school, appearing in the afternoons for the Youth or Second XV of the town team, Pembroke Dock Quins.

I made my debut for the Quins First XV one April day against Carmarthen Athletic. I was completely and humiliatingly out-hooked – it was unheard of, I normally did that to other teams, now here it was happening to me. It was so bad that one of my mates bent to stare into the tunnel between the two front rows and shouted across as we went down for a scrum near the touchline – 'Are you in there, Carradice?'

After the game one of the Carmarthen players told me I had done well to get the ball that I did. Their hooker was Norman Gale's understudy at Llanelli, playing when Gale was on Wales duty, and, had he wanted, he could have been a regular for any first-class club in the country. I can't say the information did much to restore my shattered self-confidence.

When, in my final year at school, I was made captain of the First XV I could not have been prouder, but it was not to last.

One Saturday we travelled to Whitland and managed a hard-fought draw – no mean achievement. After the game the Whitland boys suggested a quick pint in their local. Most of us were eighteen by then and we happily agreed, knowing that it was at least half an hour before the bus left.

The pub was welcoming and warm – and that's where the teacher (the same metalwork teacher who, years earlier, had stopped us playing gladiators with his cricket nets) duly found us. We were frogmarched out, much to the amusement of the Whitland lads, and on the Monday morning the whole team was hauled up in front of the Phant. 'What have you got to say for yourself, Carradice?' he screamed. 'Come on, boy, you're the captain.'

Captain at last, the school First XV in the 1966–67 season. My friend Dave
Eastick stands in the centre of the back row.

'Well, sir …,' I started.

'Stand up when you talk to me!' I stood. 'Well, sir …'

'Sit down boy,' he yelled. 'This isn't a debate!'

I gave up. The end result was that all of us who had gone to the pub – at least three
quarters of the team – were banned. It was useless to protest that we were all eighteen
years old. 'You will never represent the school again!' the Phant thundered.

It was a stupid ruling as it effectively wiped out the First XV for the rest of the
season. I carried on playing for the County and Dave Eastick went on to win his first
Welsh cricket cap, but we never played for Pembroke Grammar School again.

The only other thing I was any good at was drama. We never had drama lessons
but we invariably read plays out aloud in English literature lessons, everything from
Shakespeare and Kit Marlowe to Sheridan's *School for Scandal*. I don't know if that
was good or bad practice but the school certainly had a great reputation for its drama
productions.

A year or so before I began my 'acting career' the school had put on Peter Ustinov's
Romanof and Juliet. It was considered very risqué for a school production. Local
churches complained about the language and the fact that pupils were seen to kiss on
stage – how daring! The row rumbled on and there were even reports and comments in
the national newspapers.

Mush McCallum was in the cast and felt that, in the main, it was all a storm in
a teacup. As he later wrote, 'I thought the language was not "school play" material
– particularly a soldier suggesting that another was born out of wedlock.' It was great
fun for adolescents and it did ensure a degree of celebrity for the cast, something Mush
and the others played on for the rest of the year.

My first appearance in a school play came in *The Life of Galileo* by Bertolt Brecht.
It was not a big part, very few were in that production, which hinged totally on the

School dramatics, *The Devil's Disciple*. I am at the right edge of the photograph, my friend Phil Spencer in the centre spot.

character of Galileo, a part played with great aplomb by Michael Jones who was a year or two older than me; but my part was important – I was to play the High Official who arrested Galileo on behalf of the Vatican and, ultimately, the Inquisition.

Sammy Shaw, the producer, was clear that none of us should play rugby in the two weeks leading up to the first night. One injury and the production would be ruined. He issued an edict and expected everyone to obey. Some did but not me. There was no way I was going to miss my Thursday afternoon games lesson.

'Are you sure?' asked Dennis Lloyd, our PE teacher. 'You know what Mr Shaw said about playing games before first night.'

'I'll be all right, sir,' I shrugged. 'It's only a knock about. I'll take care.'

Of course, the inevitable happened.

Ten minutes before the final whistle I went down on a loose ball. Maxie Rickard – on my own side, would you believe? – chose that same moment to fly-hack the ball away and caught me full in the face. My eye blackened immediately and a huge swelling, green and sagging like a carbuncle exploded on my cheek. Sammy Shaw was incandescent with rage.

'See!' he bellowed, 'See! This is what happens when you don't do as you're told.'

He grabbed me by the collar of my blazer and hauled me to my feet. He pushed me to the front of the stage, in full view of the cast.

'Look at this stupid boy!' he continued to rant. 'Look at him. Now we've got a High Official of the Pope and the Holy Roman Emperor looking like he's gone fifteen rounds with Muhammad Ali.' I still think that was putting it a bit strong. A little judicious makeup and it was all OK – as long as you didn't look too closely. Anyway, I think the black eye rather suited the brutal nature of the Inquisition.

In the years that followed I took part in plays like *A Penny for a Song* by John Whiting and George Bernard Shaw's *The Devil's Disciple*. In the latter one I played something of a ladies' man – 'Type casting,' my girlfriend of the time assured me.

Best of all were the House plays. These we cast and produced on our own, without the advice or support – or, as we put it, the hindrance – of any teachers.

When it was my turn to produce, I chose a one-act farce called *On the Frontier*. It was a slight thing, taking a dig at Eastern European values and behaviours. We came second in the competition and, years later, I produced it again when I began teaching at nearby Milford. So I suppose it must have made some sort of impression on me.

On one memorable occasion I was in the cast of a one-act play called *This Desirable Cottage* – I think it was for a YFC Drama Festival. In the final scene, as bulldozers moved in to demolish the cottage, I had to appear in a nightshirt and bed cap, much to the amusement of my rugby-playing friends and girlfriend.

Best of all, however, was the response to a line I had to give. Accused of being a pavement artist who drew nudes in Sloan Square, I was to respond with 'Madam, I assure you, I have never done a nude in my life.' It drew a titter from the audience, then the loud shouted comment from somewhere at the back of the hall, 'You could have fooled me!' That one brought the house down.

A newspaper cutting of the cast of *A Penny for a Song*. I am standing second left in suitably rustic attire.

I think, in hindsight, the House plays gave us a chance to develop our artistic flair. In the big school play you had no choice but to obey the directives of the producer – Sammy Shaw or, later, Vernon Hughes – but in the house plays you were free to develop your own train of thought.

It was the same with the school magazine. The *Penvro* was an old, established magazine run by the sixth form (with teacher oversight and guidance). It was a glossy production that gave information about school teams and successes but, more importantly, it also published pieces of creative writing by pupils. It was in those hallowed pages that my first stories and articles began to appear.

One early story of mine – I can't remember what it was called – involved two secret agents trying to escape from occupied France into neutral Spain. It was '*Boy's Own*' stuff that really did reflect my reading at the time – 'Biggles' with a touch of John Buchan and Bulldog Drummond thrown in for good measure.

One man fell in the snow of the Pyrenees and broke his leg. Rather than delay or hinder his colleague he sent him off to look for help and then duly shot himself – very noble, very adolescent and, as I thought at the time, a very powerful piece of writing. In the story the other character staggered another 50 yards and fell into the arms of a Spanish border guard – safe at last.

Mush McCallum stood at the bottom of the stairs leading to the Prefects' room and solemnly shook his head. He waved his copy of the *Penvro* in the air. 'Very good, young

The cover of the Summer 1966 issue of the school magazine the *Penvro*. As well as submitting articles I also had a hand in editing this issue – well, that's one way of getting your stories published!

Carradice,' he said. 'But why did he shoot himself if they were that close to safety?'

'He didn't know,' I protested. 'He wouldn't have done it if he'd realised the border was that close.'

Mush leaned across and tapped me on the chest. He smiled, sagely. 'Then you should have made that clear.'

It was good advice, perhaps the best I have ever been offered in my writing career. I have tried, ever since, to follow a simple dictum – keep it simple, keep it clear, do nothing to confuse the reader.

The other huge influence on my writing at this time was my father. Dad was always a little careful with his money, particularly when he knew how I would waste it. When, each Friday, I would ask for ten shillings to take my girlfriend to the pictures – and you really could take a girl to the pictures for ten shillings (50p in modern parlance) in those days, and have money left over for a bag of chips afterwards – he would shake his head and frown, dubiously.

'I'm not giving you money to waste on girls,' he would say. 'Tell you what, we'll have a competition. Whoever writes the best opening to a story gets the ten bob.'

I fell for it every time. Dad, of course, was the judge and he'd carefully look at both efforts before declaring his verdict.

'Yours is rubbish. I win. I keep the ten bob.'

I was reduced to walking my girlfriends around Pembroke Dock – not something you really wanted to do on a Friday night in the cold, wind and rain. No wonder my girlfriends never lasted for long.

That's how things went on until the day I gave him this: 'There was a silence like the silence that precedes the dawn. It was as if every living creature was watching, waiting, holding its breath.' Dad looked at it and whistled under his breath, 'That's wonderful. I can't beat that. Here, have a pound.'

Until the day he died I never had the nerve to tell him that I didn't write that. It was the opening paragraph to *Biggles Sweeps the Desert* by Captain W. E. Johns, but it was my first 'paid' gig. I was on my way – even if I had cheated.

Looking back I find it amazing to consider how much luck there was in our lives – good luck and bad. Some people naturally attract misfortune and I always thought that my friend Howard must have been the most unlucky human being in the world.

Racing for the showers after a game of rugby one day he slipped on the wet floor and smashed his head on the tiles. I'd never seen anyone totally unconscious before; when we pulled him out of the showers he was like a limp rag doll. Result – one severe case of concussion and no more rugby for the year.

A few months later he, along with the rest of us, was sliding down the steep bank above the tennis courts. With the wire fencing to stop our trajectory it was great fun. Until Howard managed to find the only piece of glass on the whole bank – it must have been left over from the builders several years before.

The glass embedded itself in his leg and then carved a huge canal, from the back of his knee to the ankle. There was blood everywhere and much wailing on Howard's part, not because he'd mutilated himself, but because he'd destroyed what we all agreed were the tightest and best pair of trousers in the whole school.

Some years later Howard announced he was going to build himself a bass guitar and learn how to play. I had severe misgivings, convinced that he was going to electrocute himself. Howard duly confounded me – and everyone else – by finishing his project and then founding a rock band. He later went on to build guitars (amongst other things) for a living, so perhaps his luck had changed.

Some of the things we got up to were just outrageous. How we got away with them I'll never know – how we survived is, sometimes, beyond belief.

For a while one of the crazes was to open the windows in the geography room on the top floor of the main building and then inch along the ledge until you were able to re-enter the room by another window, perhaps 6 or 8 feet away. It was dangerous and stupid as the ledge was only 6 inches wide and the drop was at least 80 feet. If anyone had fallen, there would have been no hope of survival.

One day, as the latest volunteer – I can't remember if it was John Mason or Peter Hewitt or some other hapless individual – tottered along the ledge, somebody had the bright idea of closing both windows, leaving him stuck there and clutching at the glass like some giant stick insect.

That would have been bad enough but, at that moment Hannah Hughes, deputy head and geography teacher, came sailing into the room in her usual imperious fashion and ordered everyone to their seats. It was several minutes before, alerted by the tittering of her class, she glanced up and saw the helpless victim on the outside of the glass. The scream she gave was a combination of fear, surprise and absolute panic, but it is probably best to draw a veil over the repercussions to that particular episode.

The main school building. The geography room where disaster almost occurred is hidden behind the tree but the height of the building can be seen.

Other stupid and really mindless activities included climbing out of the ventilation windows in the roof of our coach on rugby trips – while the bus was moving. The craze didn't last long as it was too haphazard, even for us.

Then, in the days after I had passed my driving test, there was my friend Stephen Badman. His party trick was to sit behind you when you were driving and suddenly lean forward to cover your eyes with his hands. The sense of panic stays with me even today – and we all learned that if Badman was in the car with you he always sat in the front seat.

I certainly know I was lucky in the teachers who did their best to guide me through school. Too many to list, some do, nevertheless, stand out.

Dennis Lloyd, our PE teacher, was a gentle and considerate man. If anyone, it was Dennis who influenced me in my later decision to train as a PE teacher, but he did have a contradictory side to his nature. He was a lover and a renowned advocate of open rugby, of throwing the ball around at all times.

On one well-recorded occasion, we were playing against Haverfordwest, a needle match if ever there was one. They gained possession some 20 yards from our goal-line and their outside half hoisted an unexpected up and under. It wasn't a bad move and certainly not what we were expecting but Dennis promptly blew his whistle.

'What's that for?' asked the Haverfordwest captain, a puzzled and perplexed look on his face.

'You should never kick from there,' said Dennis. 'It is a total waste of possession; penalty against you.' Their captain stared at me in disbelief. I shrugged – that was Dennis.

Myself and girlfriend Elaine, taken sometime in 1965/66.

Mary Lewis, who took me for English for much of my school career, was the person who guided my reading and moved me gently away from 'Biggles' and Richard Hannay. It was through her that I encountered the writings of Dickens, Thackeray and Austen and the Welsh poet W. H. Davies, both his lyrical poetry and his prose *Autobiography of a Super Tramp*.

It was an essential widening of interest that was continued by Vernon Hughes once I entered the Sixth Form.

Vernon was nothing if not cynical. It was through him that I learned the painful lesson of backing up opinions with facts and avoiding, at all costs, sweeping generalisations. I remember, once, glibly referring to Chaucer as 'the father of English poetry' in an essay he had given me to write. Vernon turned purple and dragged me out to the front of the class to explain how I had arrived at this conclusion. I waffled on about there being no English poets before him, not really having a clue what I was talking about.

I remember Vernon's final, dismissive comment, a dagger that stuck into my heart – 'Which comic did you get that out of?' It may have hurt but never again did I make such a puerile comment.

His wife – Fireball as we called her, due to her bright red hair – was a more gentle soul but she was equally as intense in her love of English literature. She introduced me to people like Joseph Conrad and the writings of Geoffrey Chaucer have never seemed so vibrant and alive when she was extolling their virtue.

Milford Haven became, in the 1960s, the oil capital of the country. This shows the BP refinery, a place I later worked during summer vacations from college.

Chapter Nine
A Wider World

The great snows of 1963 were sudden and unexpected in their intensity. They took us all by surprise. Really, the snow began in 1962; the first flakes falling across the streets of Pembroke Dock on Boxing Day, something that really disappointed us as we had all wanted a White Christmas. However, because the snow lay on the ground until March that winter has always been designated by the simple phrase 'the Snows of 1963'.

I had never seen such snow. For months it lay 2 or 3 feet deep in Military Road and the few cars that did manage to get up and down the street soon gouged deep ruts out of the covering. The snow was thrown to the side, sometimes piling up waist-deep along the sides of the road. Some of the shapes and contours that were created by these impromptu snowploughs were spectacular.

Mind you, it made it easy for other cars – drivers simply had to follow the ruts, keeping their wheels out of the powdery snow. When it froze – as it did most nights – it looked as if the waves on the sea shore had been suspended in mid-motion.

Walking down the ruts was the best way of getting around, certainly when there was the occasional thaw and the snow fell in avalanches off the roofs of the houses. More than one of my friends found themselves suddenly engulfed by an icy white deluge when they followed the pavements. It was a miracle nobody was seriously hurt.

'Not a patch on the snow of '47,' Grampy Phillips would grumble, leaning forward to rake up the coal on the open fire. 'Then you couldn't get out of the back door. It was right up to the top of the windows.'

Yes, Grampy, I thought, and didn't believe a word of it. Only years later, when I researched that earlier snowfall for a book, did I find out he was speaking the truth. Yet knowing that, even now I find it hard to believe anything could be worse than our snowfall of 1963.

Sledging on the Barrack Hill soon replaced rugby as the sport of the moment – I don't think there was a rugby or soccer ground open for use anywhere in Wales. We built ourselves homemade sledges out of wood and spent hours greasing and treating the runners with beeswax – perhaps the most enjoyable part of the process.

Then, machines ready and suitably emboldened with a name or motif – Bob's, if I remember rightly was called the 'Rocket' – we thundered at great speed down the hill, invariably having to flop off our vehicles at the last moment to avoid the barbed wire fence that was strung across the bottom of the slope.

Ripped jeans or trousers were an acceptable part of the experience. It all went wrong when Eddie Bromhead appeared on the Hill with a brand new, custom-built sledge that his father had bought for him. Its metal runners guaranteed a speedy run and, as expected, he shot away down the slope, leaving the rest of us floundering in his wake.

Above left: The great snow of 1963 was unexpected and soon covered the town like sugar icing. Cars could barely move but young boys and girls could certainly sledge, even on roads normally out of bounds for such activities.

Above right: The town lies bandaged and white in this view from Prospect Place.

Custom-built or not, Eddie still had to throw himself from the sledge at the bottom of the Hill. It was unfortunate for him that the toboggan, low and far sleeker than our vehicles, kept going – under the barbed wire fence, down Pembroke Street, into Commercial Row and on into the distance.

The last we saw of Eddie was his back as he chased the errant sledge through town, hoping to catch it before it ended up in the waters of Milford Haven. He could have come back once he'd caught his runaway sledge, but my guess is that he just didn't have the energy.

My cousin Lawrence – Uncle Freddie's youngest son – decided it would be great fun to build two huge snow mountains in front of and behind Dad's car. Lawrence, like the rest of us, thought the snow would go after a day or so and he was not unduly worried when the snow mounds froze as solid as ice that night. In the event they were there for three months – and Dad could not use his car in all that time.

My mother was secretly quite pleased as she was sure Dad would have killed himself had he even attempted to drive in those conditions. Even so Lawrence kept well out of Dad's way the whole time the snow was on the ground – which was probably just as well, Dad would have done him a serious injury if he'd been able to lay hands on him.

It was amazing how quickly people became accustomed to the snow. To begin with it was fun, particularly for us kids. Then it became a nuisance. Within a few weeks we were so used to it that we simply accepted its presence as a part of life. Schools had been closed for the first few weeks but they soon opened again, with strict and explicit orders that pupils should not throw snowballs. At the end we were all quite pleased to see it go.

Events like the great snow of 1963 obviously impinged themselves onto our consciousness; but there were world-wide events, too, and while we were really concerned only with our own small world, sometimes we became conscious that there were great things happening out there in the 1960s.

The assassination of President Kennedy is one that I remember. They say everyone can remember where they were when they heard the news – I really can. I was on my way to the weekly Air Cadets meeting when Peter Pearce came charging along the road, calling out the news. It was quite chilling as we all wondered what the repercussions might be.

Somebody said the Russians had done it and that another world war was bound to be declared. For me there was a strange sense of acceptance. I had been listening to the radio only that morning – Jack DeManio, I think – and there had been a piece on food tasters being employed to check Kennedy's food on his Dallas trip, to make sure it was not poisoned. Who would do a thing like that, I had wondered, who would really try to kill the President of the USA?

Kennedy, of course, had championed the space race and gone on record as pledging to put a man on the moon within a decade. We followed the various space missions, from Yuri Gagarin and Alan Shepherd to John Glenn and all of the other astronauts. We stood outside in the darkness and watched as *Sputnik*, *Telstar* and other satellites cut a swathe across the night sky.

We were, we knew, witnessing marvellous things. It was only sixty years since mankind had first taken to the air and here we were, watching the first hesitant beginnings of space travel. Sometimes it just didn't bear thinking about.

Other events were rather more pedestrian, things like the death of Marilyn Monroe and the confused ramblings of the Profumo case. Who were Christine Keeler and Mandy Rice Davies, we wanted to know, and in most cases parents seemed reluctant to tell us.

The one thing we did all know about was the Cuban Missile Crisis. For a few short weeks in 1962 it really did seem as if the world was teetering on the brink of a chasm, ready to topple into the black hole of a nuclear conflict that would have engulfed us all. From the fiasco of the Bay of Pigs invasion to the eventual turning back of the Russian missile ships, we avidly followed the events as they unfolded, convinced that the end of the world was nigh. If there was any scant consolation then it came in the words of American satirist and singer Tom Lehrer, who was at least able to laugh at the situation:

We will all go together when we go,
Every Hottentot and every Eskimo.

There are those who say that John F. Kennedy mishandled the whole affair, but if he did it was the greatest mishandling of any crisis in the history of the world. The disaster was averted and we were all able to breathe easily again.

American civil rights campaigners, the songs of Bob Dylan and Joan Baez, it was an age of awakening and while, in tiny Pembroke Dock, the problems of the American Deep South sometimes seemed a long way away, we were able to identify with the struggles of people like Martin Luther King and Michael X. Books like Harper Lee's *To Kill a Mockingbird* were avidly passed between us as we struggled to understand what was going on in the supposed 'Land of the Free'.

For a long while I became quite interested in the folk scene and, in particular, in the protest songs of people like Pete Seeger, Donovan and Phil Ochs. Indeed, the Joan Baez

The Cuban Missile Crisis was one world event that we all knew about. Even today, the martyrs and heroes of the revolution are remembered in Cuba.

Climbing, always climbing, grass or rock it was all the same to me. No wonder I later took up climbing and mountaineering as a hobby.

classic 'There But for Fortune' – sung magnificently by Baez, as you would expect, but written by the unheralded Phil Ochs – became, for years, the only thing I could play passably well on the guitar.

American involvement in Vietnam was beginning to build, thanks to Kennedy's replacement, the Texan Lyndon B. Johnston, and protest against government action was a natural phenomenon.

We watched the news programmes every night, saw people in the USA burning their draft cards and wondered at the body bags that seemed to accompany every piece of newsreel from Vietnam.

Even so, I don't think I realised the full significance of what was going on until my American pen-friend wrote to tell me that her brother had just gone into the US Marine Corps and was likely to be in Vietnam inside a few months. There was no gung-ho celebration or championing of the American dream, just genuine fear that a much-loved family member would soon be in mortal danger in a country many thousands of miles away, fighting for a cause that nobody really understood or believed in. It was a sobering thought.

Pembroke Dock had always been full of characters, people who we passed in the street every day and to whom, at the time, we gave very little thought. Only with hindsight can I see them as fascinating individuals, people with stories and lives that were as compelling as any character in novels by Dickens or Tolstoy.

J. R. Williams was a famous man in town, a County Councillor and, whenDad finally became headmaster of the Coronation, his Chair of the Governors. Dad had to invite him to dinner and Mum, never at her best in such exalted company, had to steel herself for the occasion. She had always had terrible trouble with the aspirate, dropping her aitches on a regular basis.

'Practice, Mum,' I told her and watched in cruel adolescent glee as she went around the house muttering to herself – 'Do have an apple, Mr Williams.'

On the big night, after dinner was over, Mum leaned across towards J. R., proffering the fruit dish, and smiling happily, knowing her ordeal was nearly over. Calmly she said 'Do 'ave a happle, Mr Williams.' My sisters and I fell about. I don't think Mum ever forgave us for our flippancy.

Another well-known character was Smokey Joe, a man who ran the taxi service and a café in town and who we all supposed to be living on the fringes of society – although the only time I tried to sell him some copper I'd found in the school gardens he sent me away with a thick ear and a kick up the backside.

'I'll be telling your father on you,' he called as I beat a hasty retreat up the road, leaving, as I later realised, the copper on the ground outside his door.

Then there was Willie Brinn. Willie was the happiest soul around. Night and day, he would wallow down Military Road, singing at the top of his voice, impervious to weather and the taunts of supposedly 'better adjusted' individuals. Forget the Bay of Pigs or the latest smallpox outbreak, memorising Frank Ifield's latest hit was far more important to Willie.

Above all there were Snitch and Snatch. Two sisters, they lived together in what was known as Gasworks Lane – King William Street was the proper name – and they were a natural source of humour for us. Name-calling, knocking on their door and running away, we did it all. It was cruel, even brutal, but it was something we all did at one time or another.

It probably did not mean much atonement or justification, but, years later, I did try to put things right in a poem I wrote about the pair:

Snitch and Snatch we called them;
two old women, each replete
with skirts like billowing sails
and whiskers that our pre-pubescent chins
could never hope to emulate.
They haunted all our childhood dreams.

We knew that they stole children,
kept them hidden, starving
in the cellar, though naturally
none of us could offer dates and names.
They were our perfect demons.

It didn't stop us hounding, calling
"Snitch and Snatch." Or knocking, pounding
on their door, then running as they charged,
skirts flying and with banshee wails
that followed as we fled.

Until one died – we could not say which one.
Snitch – or Snatch – lived on,
shuffling a painful progress round the town.
We did not bother her – only as a pair,
one entity, could they exist.
And now their power was broken.

Except, for years, we could not
meet the milk-eyed gaze
of that survivor; ashamed,
not by what we'd said or done,
but by an emptiness that struck
as sharp as daggers in the space
Below the rib cage.
We'd watch her go and silently,
consistently, she stared us down.

One day, she seemed to promise,
one fine day...

People make communities and there were times that the people of Pembroke Dock seemed considerably larger than life. I suppose, these days, there are still characters around, people worthy of note, but somehow they seem paler, more insubstantial than those of my youth. Rose-coloured spectacles, I suppose.

Dad's great friend was the metalwork teacher in the Coronation, Harry Jones. Harry was a lovely man, a great fisherman and one of the kindest people you could ever hope to meet. He wasn't the strongest disciplinarian you'd ever seen and the kids in the Coronation were a rough, tough lot.

The door to Harry's metalwork room had a huge bronze knob. One day someone had the bright idea of heating the knob with the flame of a lighter. The class gathered round as Harry approached.

'What's the matter?' asked Harry. 'What's wrong?'

'Can't get the door open, sir,' somebody said. 'It seems to be stuck.'

Harry pushed everyone out of the way and grabbed the metal door knob. Poor Harry hit the roof – he was lucky to get away with just superficial burns.

On another famous occasion they nailed Harry's coat to the floor while he was bending down to pick up some screws or nails. Harry refused to move until they pulled out the nails – so they left him there! And yet, despite this misbehaviour you would be hard pushed to find a boy in the Coronation who did not like Harry Jones, a true gentleman if ever there was one.

Harry and Dad used to go out several evenings a week, sometimes heading for the King's Arms in Front Street, sometimes for the cricket club in nearby Crescelly. They didn't drink much and, when I accompanied them occasionally, it seemed that they spent most of the time playing the 'one armed bandit'. They rarely won and when they did Dad usually insisted that they put it all back in. 'Don't want to take the landlord's money,' he would say. Nothing I could do or say would change his mind and after a while I stopped playing the machine with him – I knew where the proceeds would be going.

Harry did try to interest Dad in fishing but it was not a sport that came easily to my somewhat hyperactive father. He did, however, manage to buy himself a boat. This was supposedly to help him and Harry get out and catch mackerel – mass suicide, I called it, as the silver-blue fish seemed to leap on the hooks whenever they were dropped in the water.

In the event Dad used the boat to joyride around the Haven. He developed a route, from the King's Arms in Front Street to the Jolly Sailor in Burton across the river, with maybe a call at Llanstadwel on the way. By careful monitoring of the tide he reckoned he could make each pub smack on its opening time.

The only times I went with him the outboard motor always seemed to break down and I would spend an hour or so rowing back to Pembroke Dock while Dad sat, confident in his captaincy, in the stern. Dad assured me that the motor never broke when he was in the boat alone – perhaps it was something to do with me, I thought.

Then, one night as we manhandled the boat up the slipway at Front Street, Dad came up with a bombshell. He was going, he said, to take the boat out to Skomer, Skokholm and Grassholm Islands. I stared at him in disbelief. 'Are you crazy?' I asked.

'Grassholm's 6 or 7 miles off shore, out in the Atlantic, for God's sake.' Dad shrugged and gestured towards his treasured craft. 'She can do it.'

Skomer, I reckoned, was just about possible although I wouldn't have fancied taking on Jack Sound, the stretch of water between the island and the mainland, at least not with his unreliable outboard motor. His boat was a tiny dingy, 10 feet long at best, fine for the harbour and sheltered water, but Grassholm was plain crazy.

I argued with him all the way home – and late into the night. Eventually he saw sense. I still think I saved my father's life that night and we finished by agreeing to see if there were any official trips out to the bird sanctuary of Grassholm. There were, on properly equipped launches operating out of Milford Haven, and Dad and I duly made the trip out to and around the island one early spring day.

An hour into the trip, about 2 miles out from land, Dad nudged me and pointed. There, just ahead of us, was a small dinghy, bow dipping and ploughing into the waves every couple of yards. The boat could not have been any bigger than Dad's and the sole occupant was already soaking. 'See,' Dad smiled. 'I knew I could have done it.'

Looking at the volume of water the dingy was shipping I was not so sure. Our skipper offered the guy a tow but he resolutely declined and ploughed on. I suppose he must have made it as, later, we heard no news of drowning and disaster, but I still think the man was mad, barking mad.

The noise of the gannets calling and screeching on Grassholm was like the roar of a battlefield and smell of guano was overpowering. I had never seen so many birds gathered together in one place. Regulations prevented us from landing and that was probably just as well – there would have been nowhere to put your feet. Of course I was seasick – if not from the motion then certainly from the smell.

'I don't know,' Dad muttered, 'Sunday sailors. You'd be sick in a rowing boat on the Mill Pond.'

I kept my counsel and said nothing but all the time thinking that maybe, just maybe, I should have let the old bugger take his planned expedition after all.

Above left: The boat on which my father and I went out to Grassholm, shown here calling at Skomer Island.

Above right: Seagulls dominate the top of Grassholm – and the smell was overpowering.

Chapter Ten
An End to Childhood

I passed my driving test when I was seventeen years old. Like most of my friends I had practiced driving on the wide, empty beach at Pendine, long before I reached statutory driving age, and had applied for my licence on the day of my seventeenth birthday.

There would be no difficulty, I felt sure. I was well used to sitting behind the driving wheel and controlling a car.

'I'll be round at seven,' I told my friends as we sat in the Prefects' Room that morning before I set out for my test. 'We'll take a trip out to Fresh West. You just make sure you're all ready.'

I should have known better. Talk about tempting providence! The trouble was, driving on a beach was very different from driving on the road. I was totally and completely over-confident and the test was an utter disaster.

I came out of the driving centre car park and turned right when the examiner had asked me to turn left. Not the best of starts. From there it went from bad to worse – I even missed my emergency stop. The sense of failure and doom when the examiner gave me the bad news was worse than failing any school exam.

I applied for a new test the same day. Thankfully, after much practice on the roads around south Pembrokeshire, it was a case of second time lucky – even though the examiner told me not to get any worse as he handed me the cherished slip of paper that informed the world I was competent enough to drive.

My grandfather would certainly not have agreed with that judgement. I came back from the test and offered to take him to the post office for his pension. Grampy turned white as we rounded the corner of Military Road on two wheels and hung onto the dashboard with knuckles that were as white as snow. He didn't say a word until we were back in the house. 'The boy's bloody dangerous,' he growled. 'Mad as a hatter. I'll never get in the car with him again.' He was true to his word. Until the day he died he steadfastly refused to accompany me, no matter how many times I offered.

Being able to drive gave me a degree of freedom I had not previously known. As more and more of my friends passed their tests we were able to expand our vision of the world outside the confines of Pembroke Dock, even outside Pembrokeshire and Wales. Of course, I would never have been able to do it had it not been for the generosity of my father.

Dad willingly surrendered the family car to my keeping. As long as I took him to school in the mornings and picked him up in the evenings, the car was mine for the day. I was supposed to put in petrol, but invariably I just called at Hughie Hall's garage and stuck the fuel onto Dad's account.

Over the next few months – while driving was still a novelty – my friends and I took regular trips to places like Cardiff and Swansea, either to watch the rugby or football or, sometimes, even to take girlfriends shopping.

In the 1960s cars became suddenly more popular – and available. Ford produced several models – Anglia, Prefect and Poplar – that were more or less identical in style and performance. Dad bought an Anglia and that was the car in which I learned to drive.

Dad had insisted I knew something about the workings of the car, how to change water, oil, tyres and so on, but my knowledge was, at best, tenuous and breakdowns were an inevitable part of motoring in those days. More than once I had to ask female passengers to take off their tights or stockings so that I could use them as emergency fan belts. I often wondered if the girls thought I got some weird or perverse pleasure out of it.

When it came to breakdowns, however, nothing even began to come close to the time I took Elaine, my then girlfriend, on holiday to see her sister in Wiltshire. The trip up to Tidworth was fine, but coming back was a nightmare.

Even allowing for the fact that there were precious few motorways in those days, a time of fifteen hours for a journey of about 250 miles has to be pretty excessive. The trouble began somewhere around Swindon when the car over-heated. It continued to do the same all the way to Cardiff with me having to stop every 20 miles or so to top up on water.

In Cardiff somebody advised me to crack an egg into the radiator as this, he said would bind up any leaks. It worked – for about 50 miles. I must have bought more eggs that journey than I have ever done since – God knows what it did to the insides of the radiator – and it was a case of stop, pour in the egg and start again all the way home. We finally got back at about midnight, cold, tired and determined never to make that trip again.

Dad's car at the time was an old Ford Anglia. It only had three gears and, more significantly, vacuum powered windscreen wipers. It meant that the harder you pressed the accelerator, the slower the wipers went – which was fine, unless you were going uphill in a rain storm!

Going uphill was always something of a problem. On one occasion I had the car full of my friends, travelling from Pembroke to the 'Dock' via the long and draining Bush Hill. With the others urging me on, I decided that the string of cars in front needed to be passed – it was just unfortunate that the driver of the car immediately in front thought exactly the same. He pulled out and, rather than abandon my manoeuvre, I decided to overtake both him and the other cars in one go.

The old Anglia was straining, every nut and bolt in the car groaning in protest as we inched past, three cars side by side on a road intended for two at the very most. Then, ahead of me and coming towards me at a rate of knots, was another car. I don't say I closed my eyes, but I certainly prayed and managed to swerve in with no more than inches to spare.

It was only when I got home that I learned my father had been a passenger in the approaching car. That little episode did manage to get me banned from the car for a couple of weeks, a punishment that did not come easily, either to me or my usually very indulgent father.

One of the big advantages of driving, of course, was that it gave you a real edge with the girls. No more standing at bus stops or walking around town in the wind and rain, now there was a warm car to sit in. It certainly made trips to Tenby or Saundersfoot a lot easier and winter Sunday afternoons watching the waves pound in onto Freshwater West beach, cuddled up in the back seat beneath a travelling rug, became one of the most pleasurable parts of late adolescence.

For what was, really, the first time I began to fully explore Pembrokeshire, all of the county from St Govan's chapel in the south to Strumble Head in the north. Some of the places, like Stack Rocks or the beach at Marloes, I had visited, perhaps, once or twice a year. Now I could go there whenever I wished. I must have put miles onto Dad's car but it was an experience I wouldn't want to change.

I can honestly say that there is nothing quite like standing on the South Pembrokeshire cliffs at sunset, watching Stack Rocks grow darker and dimmer, waiting for them to eventually merge in with the sea, only the cries of the nesting sea birds to disturb the sense of absolute tranquillity. Then, off to the pub to finish the evening.

Most of us had steady girlfriends by these final years of adolescence. It didn't stop us 'playing the field', two-timing as we called it. There was no justification for our behaviour, apart from the fact that the girls were undoubtedly doing exactly the same to us – and sometimes we did get our comeuppance.

One Saturday night I realised I had managed to double-book myself. One girl was coming by bus from the 'Dock' to Bethany Corner, the other from Pembroke – and they were both due to arrive at the same time.

By a little judicious bribery and cajoling I managed to convince my friend Barry Crawford to sit with me, waiting. I would go with the first one to arrive; he would explain and go off with the second. In the event, we sat there in the car for an hour and

Stack Rocks in South Pembrokeshire, a beautiful setting that I only began to appreciate once I learned to drive.

neither girl turned up. It was the most boring Saturday night ever – the car didn't even have a radio – and, I suppose, you could say it served us right.

For a long time we held Saturday evening parties, at least once a month. They became renowned events that everyone of our age wanted to attend, though God knows why. We were never exclusive and anyone could come – the only proviso was that you had to have a partner.

There wasn't anything special about the parties. We simply pooled our money to buy some cheap alcohol, usually sherry off the wood, and turned off the lights – photography as someone called it, turn off the lights and see what develops. With the record player stacked, you started with your partner and moved on with every new tune. In the most part it was all very innocent but you did get to kiss some lovely girls.

The cinema continued to be a draw for all of us. It certainly gave Eddie Bromhead his moment of triumph. For years he had informed us that his great uncle – or someone similar – had won the Victoria Cross. He came from an army family so we supposed he might have been telling the truth but, in all honesty, we didn't give his claims much credence.

Then out came the film *Zulu*, the story of the South Wales Borderers at Rorke's Drift during the Zulu Wars of the late 1870s. In that film Michael Caine was playing none other than Lt Gonville Bromhead. Eddie had been telling the truth all along.

Films like *Zulu* were a rarity. Usually our film fare consisted of the latest Elvis movie, *Follow That Dream* or *Fun in Acapulco*, mindless things like that. It didn't matter; we rarely saw the whole thing anyway.

The Grand Cinema, shown here shortly before its demolition. The corrugated iron roof and sides can be clearly seen.

It was in these final years of school that we discovered the beauties of small country pubs. We didn't drink a great deal, in fact nine times out of ten the driver didn't drink at all, but there was something quite special about taking a trip out to pubs like the *Salutation* near Freshwater West or the *Swan Lake* at Jameston and then sitting for an hour in front of a roaring log fire.

The *Point House* at Angle became a special favourite. It was an old smugglers' inn and when there was a high tide the sea came racing in and the place found itself cut off from the village. It was always better to be marooned at the pub, rather than at the other end of the causeway, something we tried to arrange most neap and spring tides.

I suppose, in some respects, these tiny country pubs had replaced places like Brown's or Monti's as meeting venues. They were the final stage in the growing process.

The final years of adolescence – that short and evocative time before we sailed off to university or jobs – were a bittersweet period in my life. I enjoyed my Sixth Form days – to start with I could finally study subjects that I actually liked, things like English literature and history. No more maths or languages for me. At long last, we were finally treated like adults, given a Prefects' room to sit in and actually allowed free periods – although we were supposed to use them for personal study. I used to argue that I was doing personal study, perfecting my skills in three card brag or poker, but I don't think my tutors believed me.

Inevitably, though, friendship groups that had been in existence for ten, twelve or more years began to break up. Bob and Bruce left school before taking their A-levels. Bruce joined the bank and was soon posted away. Bob went to one of the oil refineries

Paul McCartney &
George Harrison

The Beatles, role models to a whole generation, mine included.

West Angle Bay, a place where we swam, sailed and enjoyed growing up.

on Milford Haven where he rose steadily through the ranks and later went out to the Bahamas and America as a manager and junior executive. We didn't lose touch but contact was more distant, a little bit rarer – there were now other priorities.

Bob also got himself married a few years after leaving school. His wife, Anne, had been his girlfriend for years and it seemed a logical move. Their first son, Paul, is my godson, about which I still feel inordinately proud although the amount and value of advice I have offered him over the years has probably been very limited.

Bob was the first of us to settle down, buying a house and, after a while, even giving up the rock band he had played in for years. It was a symbolic moment for all of us, taking on of adult values, realising that the world would not change simply because we expected and wanted it.

There were compensations. New friends entered my life, people like Phil Spencer and Stephen Badman who transferred from the Coronation after their O-levels. I played rugby with them, partied with them and, in Phil's case, acted with him in school drama productions.

Phil was a much better actor than me and invariably took the lead while I was relegated to what you could call 'supporting roles'. It didn't stop us being friends and sharing the same back seat in the same parked cars in lay-bys or on parking spots above deserted beaches.

From girls like Caroline Hughes and Carolla Bowen I learned that members of the opposite sex were not just creatures to be used and abused, picked up and discarded at a whim, but people with minds and ideas of their own, minds and ideas that, nine times out of ten, were markedly superior to my own. They became friends, individuals with whom I could discuss things like poetry and novels at a depth I had previously only dreamed about.

For the final two years of school there was a sense of finality in the air, a feeling of closure. I noticed it first one beautiful day during that penultimate summer break.

I called in at Monti's, casually parking the car directly in front before sauntering in to wait for my friends. I waited – and kept on waiting. No-one turned up. They had all found themselves summer jobs, serving in petrol stations or labouring on one of the town's building sites. I was alone and surprisingly lonely.

I resisted the temptation to join the ranks of my working friends, at least for a few weeks, but then sheer boredom drove me to the site of the new Pembroke power station where by some miracle they took me on as a labourer.

Having lots of money in your pocket was a great feeling – but it spelled demise as far as Monti's Café and all of the other adolescent haunts were concerned. It was, I suppose, the beginning of the end.

This was the time when we also encountered death, usually for the first time. In the space of a few short years I lost both of my grandfathers. Grampy Carradice was the first to go, finally succumbing to the withering disease that had been gnawing away at his lungs for years.

His wife lived on long enough to see my own children, her great-grandchildren. They gave her the name of Nanny Donkey as her house was opposite a field of horses – and, for a young child, donkey was so much easier to say than horse. The name stuck and until the day she died she was known in the family as Nanny Donkey. She was a lovely, single-minded old lady – I just wish Grampy Carradice had been around to see and enjoy the company of my sons.

Grampy Phillips died alone, from a heart attack, when there was no-one else in the house. My sister Anne discovered his body when she came home from school one spring afternoon. He lay quietly on the settee in the living room and apart from some small ruffling of the carpet beneath his feet there was nothing to say that he was not just asleep.

Such moments were, obviously, not confined to my family. Others, I know, had similar experiences, but by now we were able to at least talk about them, in a halting, painful way. It didn't make them any easier to cope with, but there was a degree of comfort in the thought that maybe, just maybe, your friends understood what you were going through. Such deaths were uncomfortable and unexpected and did not lie easily with any of us. To some extent, though, they prepared us for the real shock that came a year or so later.

At the end of our school days Dave Eastick had gone off to university, happy and expectant like the rest of us. He and I had both returned to school for an extra year, Dave to improve his geography A-level grade, me to see if I could get some Welsh trials and maybe even a schoolboy cap. Dave did manage to improve his grade. And me? The trials happened, the cap didn't.

Dave and I became particularly close during that final year, each keeping the other going when sometimes it would have been very easy to throw up our hands in despair and head for the nearest Job Centre. As much as I enjoyed my Sixth Form days, I know I couldn't have got through them without Dave.

In due course, school finished and after one final, glorious summer it was off to college. We all looked to the future with expectation and ambition.

Then Dave contracted cancer and, inside eighteen months, he was dead. He was the first real friend I had ever lost and the pain was almost unbearable. It has never left me. Somehow, that death – even though it was a year or two after we had left school and moved on – seemed to underline the fact that childhood was now well and truly over.

When the time came to leave childhood and adolescence behind I was ready for the change, for the next stage of the journey. Growing up in a small town like Pembroke Dock had been an incredible experience and it was something to be cherished and remembered all my life – but it was not the future and I knew when I left the school gates for the last time in the summer of 1967 that I was ready to move on.